Building Digital Ecosystem Architectures

Digital technologies are revolutionizing the business world – challenging existing practices and enabling a new generation of business models.

Business in the Digital Economy is an accessible new series of books that tackles the business impacts of technology and the emerging digital economy. Aimed at non-technical, mid–senior executives and business managers, this series will help inform choices and guide decision-making on all major technological trends and their implications for business.

Series editors: Alan Brown and Mark Thompson

Available titles:

Predictive Analytics, Data Mining and Big Data
Steven Finlay
9781137379290

Building a Digital Enterprise
Mark Skilton
9781137477705

Series ISBN: 9781137395245

Building Digital Ecosystem Architectures

A Guide to Enterprise Architecting Digital Technologies in the Digital Enterprise

Mark Skilton

Professor of Practice, Warwick Business School, UK

First published 2016 by
PALGRAVE MACMILLAN

Palgrave Macmillan in the UK is an imprint of Macmillan Publishers Limited, registered in England, company number 785998, of Houndmills, Basingstoke, Hampshire RG21 6XS.

Palgrave Macmillan in the US is a division of St Martin's Press LLC, 175 Fifth Avenue, New York, NY 10010.

Palgrave Macmillan is the global academic imprint of the above companies and has companies and representatives throughout the world.

Palgrave® and Macmillan® are registered trademarks in the United States, the United Kingdom, Europe and other countries.

ISBN 978–1–137–55410–9

This book is printed on paper suitable for recycling and made from fully managed and sustained forest sources. Logging, pulping and manufacturing processes are expected to conform to the environmental regulations of the country of origin.

A catalogue record for this book is available from the British Library.

A catalog record for this book is available from the Library of Congress.

Typeset by MPS Limited, Chennai, India.

For Linda, Claire, Emma, and David.

Contents

List of Figures and Tables

╱ Tables

Foreword

Over the past century, technology – primarily in the form of computing systems – has evolved at a pace never before seen in human history. These changes have not only made life simpler for most people, but have also brought great convenience and immediacy to everyday activities. One need only to consider our new-found dependence on smartphones – devices that barely existed before the iPhone was introduced less than ten years ago in 2007 – to realize just how rapidly technology is changing our lives.

The new digital landscape has also pervaded nearly every system and organization across the globe. Despite the simplicity digitalization has brought to business processes and structures, the technology systems themselves have become increasingly complex over time. This is particularly true in large enterprises, which now require entire buildings placed strategically across globe to maintain the company "infrastructure."

To better manage these systems, enterprise architecture emerged over the past 30 years as a discipline and profession that provided a necessary bridge between the IT department and the business. It has been adopted by companies, partnerships, government departments and agencies, charities and non-profit organizations: in effect, every type of organization that exists.

Enterprise architecture addresses the complexity of information technology systems and the need to integrate new capabilities with the existing legacy in heterogeneous environments. Initially enterprise architecture was justified as a cost-saving tool. It soon moved to being recognized, not only as a means to control cost but also to enable new capabilities. Now it is becoming a critical business discipline, alongside other essential business functions such as accounting, finance, legal, or marketing, no matter whether the business is a commercial organization, a government agency or, as in the case of The Open Group, a not-for-profit enterprise.

Every organization that exists today has become its own system with a mission (whether explicit or implicit), people, processes, technology and ecosystem of partners, each of which are constantly changing at an ever increasing pace and becoming more and more complex in their own right. As such, many enterprises today are being inundated with the digitization of their business models: products and services, processes, changing costs, revenue and profit models, new subscription and incremental models in capital expenditure and operating expenses, new operating value chains and shifting market position and channels. Boundaryless Information Flow™, the vision of The Open Group, conceived over a decade ago by our members, is even more of a business imperative today, from the macro-scale of connected markets and nations to the micro-economy of trading, social media and personalized mobile services and wearables.

That vision also recognized the need for information to be secure, reliable and timely. Today, new cyber threats and challenges, together with new opportunities for e-commerce have created the need for trade-offs in the flow of information among and between organizational systems, the need for new global standards, and the need to minimize regulation, which by definition is bound by geo-political constraints.

As the march toward digitization has gained momentum, some organizations have become trapped by their brand (how they are perceived), by their culture (how they think), by their processes (how they get things done), or by their technology (in both what they make and the tools they have) and have become the victims of significant shifts in their industry. These are the areas where enterprise architecture can help organizations adapt to this new landscape.

As with any discipline, enterprise architecture also must evolve to meet the needs of the digital economy. Like other professional disciplines, enterprise architects need to adopt a culture of continuous learning. For accountants working within enterprises, the basic methods of book-keeping and accounts have hardly changed in hundreds of years, but the standards of financial reporting are constantly evolving, the needs of the business for information are constantly evolving, and the tools available to accounting professionals are constantly evolving, not to mention the complexities around taxation as governments seek to catch up and close loop-holes that have appeared as a consequence of new ways of managing an enterprise.

The tools of enterprise architects, standards such as TOGAF® and ArchiMate®, both standards of The Open Group, are relatively stable although they too will evolve over time. The real issue facing enterprise architects is how to apply standards in a world where the pace of change and complexity will only continue to accelerate. Enterprises are turning to "Agile" or "DevOps" in an attempt to accelerate their own pace of change, and enterprise architects have a valuable role to fill as part of the Scrum or DevOps teams.

Enterprises are also increasingly moving toward a new platform that represents the convergence of social, mobile, big data, cloud, and the internet of things. This new platform represents a kind of paradox that organizations will be grappling with for years to come. How can you harness this mass of data and networks and mobility to empower employees and business activity while at the same time trying to protect value, survive new digital competitors, and be able to scale and grow business performance and the value outcomes for customers, citizens, donors, members, or beneficiaries?

Both continuous learning and constant change are about remaining relevant and having an edge. For enterprise architects, the opportunities of the future lay outside of the boundaries of the current ecosystem in which we operate from day to day. This book is an important contribution to thinking about the critical role enterprise architecture must play in the new digital era.

Allen Brown
2016

Preface

In a recent conference on the future of business technology, the consensus was that if you want to build the future of a connected society then you need "to think differently," you need to adopt a "new mind set." Why is this required with the internet that emerged into the social networks and enterprise architecture in the last decade of the twenty century but is now such a major disruption well into the second decade of the 21st century?

This is the "digitization" effect that is a current theme in the modern business landscape, which is seeing significant economic and business models change as a result of digitization.

While the digital economy is still reportedly seen as only 6 percent to 11 percent of GDP in terms of e-commerce transactions, market survey trends point to 30 percent to 40 percent of revenue growth from digital channels alone across local and global marketplaces. Driven by massive mobile and social media growth rates taking hold in society, the emerging digital behavior is shifting to even larger rates of 60 percent to 70 percent in terms of movement of business processes and data into digital product and services and new digital operating models.

Every day we experience and see the effects of digitization in the lowering of barriers to entry from search engines to the accessibility of degrees of freedom that enable online purchases, digital payments, streaming movies and music to rapid social network connectivity and data insight. Yet this knowledge of physical transformation does not consider the virtualization effects that digitization brings with it, enabling concurrency of multiple tasks, co-presence of people and connections who may be thousands of miles apart. A new kind of digital convergence and entanglement is emerging that a generation ago would have been limited to singular transactions, technically cost prohibitive, or just plain unthinkable.

Today the Enterprise Information Systems Landscape is a combination of the new and old technologies. IT infrastructures consisting of networking, data centers, and devices have come to define the modern enterprise platforms that run sales and marketing, operations, planning, and productivity software applications. Yet practitioners in both IT and business have been faced with enormous changes in how enterprise solutions are brought into the organization and their ability to spread from inside and reach outside the company boundaries. The rise of the term "digital technologies" and "digital transformation" have led the way in describing social media, big data, mobile devices, and cloud computing in reinventing how customer experience (CX) and user experience (UX) can be developed and enhanced. The large-scale enterprise platforms seen in examples such as ERP, CRM, PLM, SCM, SRM, Office productivity, email, and website content have undergone major technological changes driven by the new capabilities of technologies that have created new virtual workplaces, virtual reality (VR), embedded Internet of Things, machine learning (ML) and artificial intelligence (AI), to new augmented systems that transform customer experience and new capabilities.

This is the "digitization effect" driving new consumerization, crowds, and ecosystems where value and loyalty are increasingly based on the level of connected and shared experience.

This book seeks to explore the ways in which enterprise architecture considers how different types of technological and business ecosystems are designed and constructed with digital technologies. We examine how the scope of enterprise systems is increasing, driven by connected digital technologies that span the enterprise both internally and externally. This is changing how enterprise architecture needs to think and work effectively for customers, employees, businesses, and the wider society of the digital economy.

A "different mindset" is a reality, but this will not happen by magic and will need a new "architecture" approach to build the digital ecosystems of the new digital connected economy.

Mark Skilton
2015

Acknowledgments

The development of this book has involved many hours of research and interviews with professional practitioners and academics in the field of business and information technology. I would like to give recognition and sincere thanks to the following people who gave their time in discussions, sharing thoughts, and ideas that have helped me to craft this book. Simon Ricketts, Group CIO of Rolls-Royce; Simon Bedford, Associate Producer (Digital), Warwick Arts Center; Geraldine Calpin, Senior Vice President and Global Head of Digital, Hilton International; Gary Lyon, Chief Innovation Officer, MasterCard Labs, MasterCard Worldwide; Matthew Hanmer, Global Product Development, Consumer Products, MasterCard Worldwide; Sybo Dijkstra, Senior Director, Philips Research, UK; Peter Latham, VP Logistics, Coca-Cola Enterprises; Mark Elkins, Head of Digital Sales and Marketing, Coca-Cola Enterprises, and Lesley Tout, Supply Chain Systems Director, Coca-Cola Enterprises; Alan Welby, Executive Director of Liverpool City Local Enterprise Partnership; Daniel Goodwin, Executive Director of Finance and Policy at the Local Government Association, and Chief Executive of St Albans City & District Council; Dr Alex Roy, Economist, New Economy, Manchester City Council; Ulf Venne, Senior Manager, Customer Engagement, DHL; Alison Crook, General Manager of Supply Chain HSS, Unipart Logistics; Professor Joe Nandhakumar, Information Systems and Management, and Assistant Dean, Warwick Business School, University of Warwick, UK; Professor Ola Henfridsson, Information Systems and Management and Head of ISM faculty, Warwick Business School, University of Warwick, UK; Vikas Vishnoi, Full-Time MBA, Warwick Business School, University of Warwick, UK; Professor Irene Ng, Marketing and Service Systems, and

Director of the International Institute for Product and Service Innovation at WMG, University of Warwick, UK; Dr Susan Wakenshaw, Research Fellow, WMG; Xia Mao, Senior Research Fellow, WMG; Allen Brown, President and CEO of The Open Group; Dr Chris Harding, Director of Interoperability, The Open Group; Jacqui Taylor, CEO of FlyingBinary; Shaon Talukder, CEO of GeoTourist; Ben Waller, Senior Researcher, ICDP; Dr Vinay Vaidya, Chief Technology Officer, KPIT; Rupert Fallows, Services Business Development, KIPT; Professor Christopher James, Director, Warwick Engineering in Biomedicine, School of Engineering, University of Warwick, UK.

Many thanks also to the Palgrave Macmillan series editors; Professor Alan W. Brown, Associate Dean, Entrepreneurship and Innovation, Surrey Business School, University of Surrey, UK; and Dr Mark Thompson, Senior Lecturer Information Systems, Cambridge Judge Business School, University of Cambridge, UK; and to Palgrave Macmillan for the opportunity to contribute to this series.

A special thanks to Allen Brown for his kind support and the Foreword; and to chapter contributor Geraldine Calpin, who has been immensely helpful. Also a big thank you to my script reviewers Dr Chris Harding, Forum Director of Interoperability at The Open Group; Philipp Kukai, PhD researcher in digital strategy at the Information Systems Group at Warwick Business School, UK, and Vikas Vishnoi, full-time MBA, Warwick Business School, UK and co-founder of Aevesto Technologies. Also a personal thanks to Vladimir Banarek for great discussions on the meaning of ecosystems; and to Penelope Gordon for her invaluable insights in product strategy monetization and metrics.

I would like to add a personal thanks to Professor Mark Taylor, Finance and Dean of Warwick Business School; Professor Andrew Lockett, Strategy & Entrepreneurship and Deputy Dean; Professor Joe Nandhakumar, Information Systems and Management, and Assistant Dean, Warwick Business School; and Professor Ola Henfridsson, Information Systems and Management and Head of ISM faculty, Warwick Business School, University of Warwick, UK, for their kind support and my endeavors at Warwick Business School.

Many thanks to all the contributors to the book and to all my colleagues and friends who have supported me over the years, it means a great deal to me. I hope this book provides some justice for all our efforts – and to those who seek to make an original thought leadership contribution and recognize the importance of respect for professional competency-led practitioners in this important and exciting revolutionary time in technology.

About the Author

Mark Skilton is Professor of Practice in Information Systems and Management at Warwick Business School. With over 20 years' experience in information technology in many commercial and public sector businesses, he specializes in helping companies realize their business value, covering social media networks, big data, mobility, machine to machine (M2M), internet of things (IoT), and cloud computing. He has worked with some of the top global international companies at board level to realize their vision of digital operating models across their complete technology landscapes. Mark is now Digital Leader at PA Consulting and, prior to that, was Global Director of Strategy at Capgemini. Previously, Mark was European CTO of services, outsourcing, and strategic technology consulting solutions at CSC. He has been Head of Digital business analysis at BSkyB TV and media company; led business re-engineering engagements at KPMG Consulting, and worked in transforming the business and IT of companies in over 25 countries worldwide. Since 2010 Mark has held international standards body roles in The Open Group, where he was co-chair of cloud computing and leading open platform 3.0 initiatives and standards publications. Mark is active in the ISO JC38 distributed architecture standards and in the "Hubs-of-all-things," a multidisciplinary project funded by the Research Council's UK Digital Economy Programme. Mark is also active in cyber security forums at Warwick University, Ovum Security Summits, and INFOSEC. He has spoken at the EU Commission on Digital Ecosystems Agenda and is an EU competition judge on Smart Outsourcing Innovation. Mark has an MBA, as well as a post-graduate qualification in production engineering and design management from Cambridge University and a degree in applied engineering science subjects from University of Sheffield.

Notes on Contributors

Allen Brown

Allen Brown is President and CEO of The Open Group – a global consortium that enables the achievement of business objectives through IT standards. He is also President of the Association of Enterprise Architects (AEA).

Allen was appointed President & CEO in 1998. Prior to joining The Open Group, he held a range of senior financial and general management roles both within his own consulting firm, which he founded in 1987, and other multi-national organizations.

Allen is TOGAF® 9 certified, an MBA alumnus of the London Business School and a Fellow of the Association of Chartered Certified Accountants.

Geraldine Calpin

Geraldine Calpin is Senior Vice President and Global Head of Digital at Hilton Worldwide, responsible for setting the strategic direction for Hilton's digital guest agenda, and maximizing commercial advantage from all direct digital channels. She joined Hilton Worldwide in 2002. During her tenure, she has been responsible for the launch of Hilton's pioneering digital check-in with room selection solution at over 4,000 hotels, the introduction of its e-commerce function, and the development of its unique e-commerce and demand generation program for hotels globally. Prior to joining Hilton Worldwide, she held various roles within the travel industry, including sales, planning, operations, and marketing roles at Trusthouse Forte and Le Méridien Hotels.

List of Abbreviations and Acronyms

ACID	Atomicity, consistency, isolation, durability
ADAS	Advanced driver assistance
Additive Manufacturing	3D printing
AGI	Association for geographical information
AI	Artificial intelligence
AIT	Automated identification technologies
ALM	Application lifecycle management
API	Application program interface
ARPU	Average revenue per user
ATM	Automatic teller machine
ATTE	Advanced technology transformation engineering
AUM	Assets under management
B2B	Business to business
B2C	Business to consumer
BASE	Basically available, soft state, eventually consistent
BC	Business continuity
BEPS	Base erosion and profit shift
Bluelight	An anti-terrorism force
BPM	Business process management

C2B	Consumer to business
C2C	Consumer to consumer
C2P	Content to purchase
CAD	Computer-aided design
CAM	Computer-aided manufacturing
CDO	Chief data officer
CDO	Chief digital officer
CEO	Chief executive officer
CGI	Computer-generated image
Churn	The rate of change of customers arriving and leaving your product or service
CIO	Chief information officer
CMB	Contact memory button
CMO	Chief marketing officer
CSO	Chief security officer
CRM	Customer relationship management
CVaR	Calculated value at risk expected shortfall
CX	Customer experience design
DDOS	Distributed denial of service (cyber attack)
DEco	Digitally-enabled ecosystems thinking
DoD	Department of Defense
DOM	Digital operating model
DOVE	Digital operating value ecosystem
DR	Disaster recovery
DSN	Deep space network
EA	Enterprise architecture
eCitizen	The use of digital technologies to support society and citizens
eGovernment	The use of digital technologies to develop government administration and citizen services

eHealth	Electronic-enabled health
EPC	Electronic product code
ERP	Enterprise resource planning system
EU	European Union, the European Commission
EV	Electric vehicle
FMCG	Fast-moving consumer goods
FRS	Fire and Rescue Services
GDP	Gross domestic product
Geofencing	The ability to track and send notifications to users when in a location
GLAS	Global logistics application suite
GODI	Ghana government open-data website
GPS	Global positioning satellite
GRC	Governance, risk and compliance
GUI	Graphical user interface
GVC	Global value chains
H2H	Human-to-human interface
H2M	Human-to-machine interface
HFT	High-frequency trading
HIPPA	Health Insurance Portability and Accountability Act
HMO	Health maintenance organization (Israel)
HPC	High-performance computing
Hypercloud	A term referring to super scale investment in data center and network infrastructure
IAN	Inter-continental global area network
IATA	International Air Transport Association
iBeacon™	A trademark for an indoor positioning system by Apple Inc.
ICDP	International car distribution program
IGPM	Institute of Governance & Public Management, Warwick Business School, UK

IMF	International Monetary Fund
IO	Input–output
IoT	Internet of things
IP	Intellectual property
IP	Internet protocol address
IPCC	Inter-governmental panel on climate change, UN
ISP	Internet service provider
IS	Information system
ISS	International Space Station
IT	Information technology
ITESs	Information technology-enabled services
IXP	Internet exchange point
LEP	Local Enterprise Partnership, UK government
LiSi	Levels of information systems interoperability
LAN	Local area network
M2H	Machine to human interface
M2M	Machine-to-machine interface
MAN	Municipal area network
MES	Manufacturing execution system
Metadata	A set of data that describes and gives information about other data
mHealth	Mobile-enabled health
Mi	More Independent, UK government technology strategy board initiative
ML	Machine learning
MOOC	Massive open online course
MSP	Multi-sided platform
NATO	North Atlantic Treaty Organization
NFC	Near-field communication

NGO	Non-governmental organization
NHS	National Health Service, UK
NSP	Network service provider
OECD	Organisation for Economic Co-operation and Development
OEM	Original equipment manufacturer
OP3	Open Platform 3.0™, The Open Group
OWL	Web Ontology Language Semantics and Abstract Syntax
PAM	Personal ambient monitoring
PAN	Personal area network
Pareto	An economic principle of inequality of inputs and outputs, 80:20 rule
PAYG	Pay-as-you-go
PCST	Privacy, confidentiality, security, and trust
PDM	Product data management
PEC	Physical, extended, contextual model
PIM	Product information management
PLC	Programmable logic controller
PLM	Product lifecycle management
PSS	Product-service system
QR Code	Quick response code
Ramsey price	Variation of marginal cost pricing based on scarcity of products and resources
RFID	Radio frequency identification
SCM	Supply chain management
SDK	Software development tool kit
SEC	US Securities and Exchange Commission
SKU	Stock-keeping unit
SmartCity	The use of digital technologies to enable citizen services in city living spaces and efficiencies

SoSi	System of systems integration
SRM	Supplier relationship management
ST	Structuration theory
STC	Spatial, temporal, contextual model
STS	Sociotechnical system
Telecare	The remote support of healthcare to patients and assisted living services
Thin provision	Demand over allocation method to optimize utilization
TIFF	Tagged image file format
TMS	Transport management system
TRM	Technology reference model
Ts & Cs	Terms and conditions
TSN	Terrestrial satellite service
TSP	Two-sided platform
UN	United Nations
UNPACS	United Nations Public Administration Country Services
USEFIL	Unobtrusive Smart Environments for Independent Living
UX	User experience design
V2V	Vehicle-to-vehicle
VaR	Value at risk
VC	Venture capitalist
VMI	Vendor-managed inventory
VNE	Value network ecosystem
VO	Virtual organization
VPN	Virtual private network
VRM	Vendor relationship management
WAN	Wide area network
WBS	Warwick Business School, University of Warwick, UK

WEF	World Economic Forum
WHO	World Health Organization, UN
XDI	Internet exchange point
Wi-Fi	Wireless network
WLAN	Wireless area network
WMG	Warwick Manufacturing Group, University of Warwick, UK
ZDI	Zero-day initiative

Book Structure

The design of digital solutions has become a pressing concern for practitioners faced with a plethora of technology impacting their business. From cloud computing to social networks, mobile computing and big data to the emerging of Internet of Things, enterprise products and services, the rooms and buildings that are connected to the wider ecosystem of networks and services are changing. This book aims to outline a distinct approach. Firstly, it seeks to explain how these digital ecosystems are defined, using examples from real industry cases. Secondly, it shows how enterprise architecture is evolving to address the connection to User Experience (UX), Customer Experience (CX), and the digital workspaces that connect these physical organizations with the virtual enterprise.

The scope of the book covers architectural concepts and design features used in developing digital technologies in mobile, cloud computing, social network media, big data, Internet of Things sensors, machine learning, and cyber security. A working definition of digital workspaces is provided as an architectural building block for a digital enterprise, illustrated with working examples from many industry case studies. The evolution of enterprise architecture practices are explored in the development of digital platforms to enable physical and virtual social and material object collaboration and experience. We identify emerging digital design patterns and see the emergence of ecosystem architecture concepts to enable market-making of digital enterprise activity and how digital technologies are clustering, and moving competition to the digital ecosystems level.

Among its most distinctive features, the book provides:

- A workable technical definition of a digital enterprise and digital ecosystems.
- An extensive discussion on digital design using converging technologies of social media networking, mobility, big data, cloud computing, and M2M Internet of Things sensors.
- A novel new approach to designing enterprise architecture using digital workspaces that drive payback outcomes.
- An expanding set of techniques and digital design patterns from cross-case analysis to illustrate successful design methods for building digital enterprise and digital ecosystems in the digital economy.

These features are important in understanding the impact of digitization on enterprise architecture and the challenges for people and organizations trying to build and grow their digital enterprise. Following the definitions to digital ecosystems and the use cases, the book has two extensive and important chapters pertaining to identifying and making sense of physical working environments and turning them into successful digital workspaces. This is followed by specific techniques for how these workspaces become digital platforms and examples of digital design patterns. The purpose of this provides a connective flow between strategies to the architectural design using digital technologies.

The book seeks to appeal to a professional and academic audience involved in the strategic planning, design, and implementation of digital enterprise architectures. The focus of the text is on the lessons drawn from cross-case analysis and from direct experience of practitioners in the field. Each chapter defines an insightful set of characteristics associated with digital ecosystem solutions success.

The sequence of the chapters deliberately follows a linear flow from understanding the digital ecosystem concepts in Chapter 1, which helps bound the scope that we explore in the book and frames the case examples in industries. We then introduce a novel way of understanding the digitization of physical workplaces into workspaces that use technologies in Chapter 2 and then illustrate how this enables ecosystem architecture design approaches in Chapter 3, supported by real case study examples. The book provides an analysis and set of lessons learnt in enterprise architecture practices designing key digital workspaces using technologies that make up a digital enterprise to achieve successful payback outcomes.

Disclaimer

All company names, trade names, trademarks, trade dress designs/logos, copyright images, and products referenced in this book are the property of their respective owners. No company references in this book sponsored this book or the content thereof.

Introduction

Practitioners in the Digital Era

This book aims to provide a practitioner's perspective of what it is like to develop the next generation of information technology (IT) solutions that will computerize corporate enterprises.

The focus is on examining how enterprise architecture has changed in recent years as the evolving phenomenon called "digitization" has taken place. We will look at examples of "thinking digitally" in this new era of the digital economy, which is characterized by hyperconnectivity and rapidly scaling technologies and systems.

I hope this is also a primer for what it means to "be digital," and will clearly show the impact and expanding influence of technology not just on business practice but also on the wider ecosystem of society and everyday life.

I believe that a *shift in mindset* is required in today's world, and this is one of the key motivations that drove me to develop the ideas and concepts that have emerged, supported by a myriad of case studies. Digitization changes physical space, time, content, meaning, and usage of information into a new kind of virtual space. This book will explore real practical examples and the limits of this digitization impact, and will identify how technology-enabled solutions can construct new realities with social and economic potential.

Whether you are seeking to market a new physical or digital product, or you are the head of a city planning organization that is seeking new skills and technology investment, or a research and development scientist developing new medical drug treatments, you will be seeking outcomes that can be radically changed by effective investment in technology and its integration with people's daily lives. Understanding and defining effective digital architectures and infrastructures, and the act of architecting effective digital solutions, are at the core of this journey.

Architecture Practice

The *Oxford English Dictionary* definition of architecture is the "complex or carefully designed structure of something." A computer science version of architecture is "the conceptual structure and logical organization of a computer or computer-based system." The ISO international standards systems and software engineering definition of architecture focuses on the act of specification of architecting as a "formal description of a system, or a detailed plan of the system at component level, to guide its implementation," and relates to the standard ISO/IEC 42010:2007.

All these definitions touch on aspects of defining a structure with meaning. Technology architecting is not just the preserve of IT practitioners but relates to a wider canvas of business and technology players. People, processes, and technology have to work together. Digital technology is a pervasive adoption and innovation process that transcends local specifications to create a rich picture of objects, actors, events, platforms, and environments. This suggests a wider ecosystem definition that we will explore in order to define capabilities and practices. This broader definition is as follows[1]:

Definition of architecture

The structure of components, their interrelationships, and the principles and guidelines governing their design and evolution over time

In considering digital technologies, the practitioner has to use a broader definition of architecture in order to encompass the digital ecosystems that populate the world today. The idea of Enterprise Architecture (EA) is not just a set of architectural building blocks from within the organization, but a structure that includes user experience and the whole ensemble of techniques and solutions that exist today in the digital world. An ecosystem perspective of architecture therefore includes many solutions and technologies.[2]

This perspective may be arrived at in an enterprise via many routes, involving both business and technical skills and leadership. We explore the building of digital solutions by focusing on examples taken from practical case studies that involve practitioners in leading organizations who are seeking to use and develop technologies for better economic performance and outcomes. We describe the techniques that these practitioners can teach us, and seek to define principles and good practices in the development of digital enterprise in the emerging digital economy.

System of Systems Integration

My intention in using a broad architectural definition is to cover both *open* and *closed* systems of exchange and services. In many cases, because of a variety of technical compatibility limitations and for operational reasons, IT systems may not be connected directly together, thereby working in an isolated manner. This may be deliberate or just because of circumstances. The concepts of *portability* and *interoperability*, which are central ideas in the exchange of information and services, underlie the designing of technologies that can work effectively across many devices and networks.

From pioneering practitioner work at the Department of Defense in the US, and at NATO in Europe in conjunction with the Software Engineering Institute at Carnegie Mellon University, from about 2003 to 2009, ideas emerged concerning System of Systems integration (SoSi) and Levels of Information Systems Interoperability (LiSi).[3] These were early forerunners of the ideas about thinking across systems, and originated in the planning of military operations. The aim was to establish an overall plan of command and control capability in a battlefield theater. The ability to link systems allows officers and the command structure to coordinate different tactical and strategic fighting units. While each unit could still operate independently under a common command set of rules, it could easily join with others and collaborate when necessary.

An open system may choose connections with other systems through standard protocols so that they can understand and communicate with each other. *Interoperability* is the concept whereby exchange of information across many systems that may be in different locations or languages can work and act as if they were one single system through the imposition of common standards. *Portability* is the ability to move information from one system to another without interfering with its operation. Both interoperability and portability are important features of system of systems thinking that have enabled new forms of architecture to evolve.

The idea of *tight* and *loose* coupling is a key concept that defines the ability of systems to connect directly and formally or to work independently and loosely. Control may be tightly coordinated or distributed between autonomous units. This is critical in scenarios where multinational armed forces which are working together speak in different languages and work with different military assets. The idea of connecting as a cohesive network is critical. Connecting in this manner also underpins the concept of interoperability, whereby different units from different countries and land, sea, air, and cyber defense can work as a joined-up set of services (see Figure i.1).

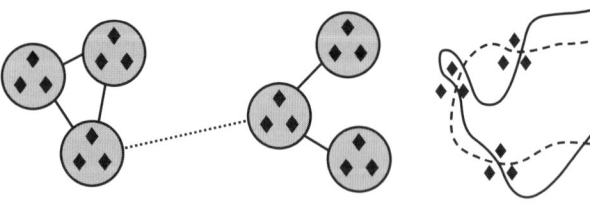

Tight and loose coupling within system of systems   **Network of interoperable services**

FIGURE i.1 / Early system of systems concepts – DoD, NATO, Carnegie Mellon 2003–9

Considerations like this allow us to take an important step in systems thinking, in which distributed complex systems can be described as a "system of systems":

> *System of systems*
>
> Large-scale concurrent and distributed systems, the components of which are complex systems themselves

In the digital world there are many cases where digital technologies connect and collaborate as a tightly or loosely coupled system of systems. Social network platforms bring together many types of communities that share and exchange information through a variety of mobile devices and websites. While none of the mobile devices are connected directly through the social network, they are part of a common set of information that may either be open to the public or private, or shared among selected friends or enterprises. The interoperability of mobile devices works at a simple level through the common syntax of internet URLs and v4 or v6 IP addresses, which enable connectivity. Devices may come from different manufacturers and use different operating systems or software applications, but they can in most cases share data and messages. Digital marketplaces have formed as a result of these common properties, and levels of control are exerted formally or informally by enterprises that control new members or new technology devices as they arise.

A key difference between these marketplaces and the internet is that in a sense there is no single command and control system of the internet. In many digitized social networks and marketplaces, enterprise owners exert their own policies and control over the membership. Other networks on the internet may be open to anyone, with no overall control. The internet might be considered open, just with common standards for internet address protocols and messaging to enable common communication. While governments, ISPs, telecoms, and service providers can exert control over parts of these systems, there is nevertheless a general system of systems. The degree to which systems are open or closed is very much dependent on investment, whether interested parties decide to work together, and which technologies are chosen.

System of Systems thinking in digital ecosystems is a network of devices, objects, connections, and services that represent the digital world and its many workplaces.

Value Network Analysis and Social Graphs

Establishing systems of systems involving digital technologies has changed the value of networks that are created and has also affected the formation of social networks. The definition of value in a digital network is recognized as being more than just economic and financial, but can also include social value, knowledge, and other non-material values. In addition, physical connections are not limited to one-to-one or one-to-many, as in the physical world, but can be many-to-many in the digital world.

This many-to-many relationship pattern represents a shift from a "value chain" to a "value network" type of thinking, which recognizes the nature and complexity of the manifold physical and virtual connections. Social graphs have evolved to map social connections, behaviors, and the preferences of these many-to-many relationships to gain insights into and make inferences about human and system behavior patterns. Our "likes" and "dislikes" are made directly or indirectly apparent by the way we interact and associate with content, websites, people, and messages on the digital network. A "digital smoke trail" is left behind, which gives clues and direct information about what we may value, whom we spoke to and when, where we interact, the brands and social preferences we acknowledge, and so on. Digitization has created a new and unprecedented level of awareness. This in turn has enabled a new kind of information analysis, which has enabled targeted advertising and other recommendations, as well as other personalization. This has the downside of affecting personal privacy, confidentiality, and the extent to which operations and services are trusted or viewed as secure. Our social networks become tangible evidence of our connections and activities. In business enterprises, similarly, an intangible network of value that surrounds the organization can form indirect associations with customers and suppliers and their social connections.

The modern digital enterprise lives in the value networks that connect across customers, employees, and partners. Social and organizational collaboration, trading, and analysis can be conducted through relationships that are defined physically and by digital technologies. The enterprise value operating model can be defined through its tangible and intangible knowledge and collaboration networks both inside and integrated with the wider marketplace and the enabling technologies of mobile, social media, and cloud ecosystems. Tangible value is defined by company information, management and employee reporting lines, and skills and expertise inside and outside the organization. Intangible knowledge networks are the informal associations and tacit knowledge that exist in the minds and experience of employees and value connections.

Semantics and Contextualization

The explosion of digitized content has led to a wide variety of digital information ways. From early web pages with their basic text and images we have moved to fully integrated websites that include video, voice, and other data, such as geographic positioning, ecological, environmental and biological information (geospatial maps, 3D drawings, biological and physiological data), as well as virtual reality and other digital information. From a practical standpoint, many efforts have been made to establish tagging and other index systems to codify a common notation of the meaning of objects. Indeed, the idea of semantics has been to introduce common standards to text, images, and everyday objects in order to enable machine-readable data services. Search engines are sophisticated enough today to discover similar text within web pages and online books, as well as similar images and soundtracks. Voice recognition and image recognition are now routinely used in call centers and airports – including passport controls in some countries. Computing machines can now mimic spoken language and basic questions, but within a set of algorithms. It is a quest of digitization to use information in context, in the moment of information sharing and when and where individuals need that information: without understanding the meaning of information, it is less easy to share it and use it purposefully. The classification of an object such as a hotel and its rooms becomes of increasingly higher value to the enterprise and its users as the information is used in context.

All these trends point toward the use of "information in context." The goal is perhaps to understand the context of objects and their uses so that humans and machines might be able to better gauge the meaning of each situation to enable higher value outcomes.

This is a central idea for practitioners who attempt to define the true meaning of a "thing" or an "event" in the location where an individual or an enterprise is to be found. Context is necessary if information and relationships are able to communicate with and understand one another. Contextualization occurs when objects and activities are "in context" and immediately meaningful. It is also a wider prerequisite to understanding needs and interactions, thereby allowing "influence at a distance." By this I mean that a common language is necessary to work across distributed locations, devices, objects, and people: locations that are half the world away (physically) from each other can cultivate mutual understanding via digital technologies.[4]

Changing Architecting Paradigm

For thousands of years, goods and services have been traded in person and through markets, but this has changed profoundly in recent living memory through the advent of IT and communications. Now it is not just products that can be traded, but technologies, interconnections, and services as well. This technological revolution has developed beyond the four walls of organizations to encompass how humans measure and interact, in minutes and milliseconds, every hour of the day and every day of the year. It impacts how social groups form and exchange knowledge and ideas; how transportation and energy are managed and sustained; how everyday objects, buildings, and whole living environments can be automated and augmented with intelligence; and even changes how cities, countries, and regional identity operate.

Human presence, our social and commercial relationships, and the locations in which we live and work, are no longer constrained to the physical realm but can be experienced virtually through the effects of "digitization."[5] Early academic research described "new media objects" such as image, voice, and digital data as expanding digital data in communications and media studies.[6] It was realized that data was not limited to the transcription of paper and transactional content into bytes that were then shared over networks and web pages, but that sound and imagery were also part of the interconnected world, thereby creating a much richer experience. This research rapidly expanded into digital artifacts and digital infrastructures and the development of mechanisms that scaled the use of digital into large platforms,[7] which is becoming evident in the growth of social media networks that emerged in the early 2000s.[8] Other academic research saw the effects of digitization on the codifying of culture and behavior into digital artifacts.[9] This meant that human expressions of social meaning and relationships could form communities of association, whether informal clusters of common interest or formal clubs, business associations, or trading markets. Different demographic groups and other types of information and choices could be recorded and analyzed. Later research, by governments, corporations, and academics, has seen major changes in the nature of the control of information, which has impacted on the economy and on economic activity.[10] Digitization has disrupted whole industries, such as travel, books, media, and banking, and potentially has an impact across all market sectors as new forms of commercial digital operating models arise.[11] National and industrial security have also changed dramatically, with the advent of cyber threats and privacy attacks raising general awareness of the need for cyber security.[12] Technology innovations have created new computing fields, such as machine learning and artificial intelligence through cognitive computing,[13] developments which are further changing how information can create and adapt new knowledge and insight in the context of particular situations and locations.

These are just a few of the themes that some observers call "game changers" that are to be found in the "digital ecosystem," and every one of them has profound consequences. From a practical perspective, it is essential to observe how these changes are combining across social, business, and human activities. From the point of view of a practitioner, it is clear that these new trends present both opportunities and challenges for enterprise and the new digital economy.

New Worlds in Motion

It is important to point out that the digital revolution is not limited to the digital technology of bytes and semiconductors. Emerging innovations in nano-technology, fiber optics, photonics, quantum, and generic engineering, for example, are changing how technology can be used. Much of the research today, in industry and in universities alike, is active in the boundary between computation and many other disciplines, such as engineering, medicine, social and cognitive learning, robotics, the financial world, and statistics simulation – to name just a few. The term "digital" in this sense is a catch-all for the conversion of physical recording and processing of information into a convertible form of virtual information, which has radically different characteristics and attributes from the physical world.

We have passed a point of no return in the digitization of data, with early technology no longer placing any limits on us. We are in a new technological era in which an information-driven economy will continue to have profound implications for jobs, economic development, creativity and innovation, competitive advantages, security, and ethics.

Crossing the Rubicon – the Digital Continuum

The last hundred years have seen profound technological developments that are redefining the boundaries of business and the markets. The first transatlantic cable was laid a century and a half ago, in 1856, and operated for three weeks.[14] Short-wave radio for transatlantic communication was established by 1927,[15] but it was not until the late 1950s that technological advances enabled practical voice communication for commercial development. Today this has radically changed, with data networked through the vast infrastructure of terrestrial, satellite, and network investments that span the globe.

As Mark Newman points out in the introduction of his book about networks, "It is important not to confuse the internet with the world wide web."[16] The internet is the physical infrastructure, while the world wide web is a packet-switching data network using a common standard known as the Internet Protocol (IP).

From a digital practitioner point of view this is one of the basic foundations for many of the innovations and structures that are termed the digital infrastructure. The hierarchy of the internet "backbone" and its various tiers of networks represents the concept of *internetworking* that enables many networks to talk and to exchange information. The internet is a "network of networks" framework of technologies and standards that enables resources to be shared and distributed across different domains of the network. Tier 2 and Tier 3 network service providers, or ISPs, enable much of the front-end connectivity to the network users.

The development of the scope of internetworking as an expanding continuum of different layers of telecommunications networks and protocols, and the fixed and mobile devices and sensors that are increasingly connected and populating this digital universe:

- The networking continuum (see Table i.1)
- The device and sensors continuum (see Table i.2).

The digital perspective is the data centers, devices, and data that reside in these networks, and how they enable users and enterprises. It is this second level of connectivity between networks and devices and the sensors across these, in what I describe as the *digital continuum*, that involves different network protocols and devices and sensors that are starting to create the technological ecosystem and the digital enterprise within it. Examples of these include network topologies, which typically represent the physical area of network span, not necessarily coverage (which is a function of transition power, terrain, and other factors). Spectrum frequencies, and device and network protocols are examples of the way in which the electromagnetic spectrum is split up commercially for different communications usage. On top of these protocols there is a large amount of security and usage legislation that is designed to control access to and the certification of services.

Examples of network topologies

TABLE i.1   Network topologies

DSN	Deep-space networks
Various	Military, commercial, dark, off-band
TSN	Terrestrial satellite service networks, media, GPS
IAN	Intercontinental global area networks
MAN	Municipal area networks
WAN	Wide area networks
WLAN	Wireless area networks
LAN	Local area networks
PAN	Personal area networks
VPN	Virtual private network

Examples of device and sensor receiver and transmission networks

TABLE i.2   Spectrum frequency – device receiver and transmission network protocols

Mobile cellular networks	5G testing 12 Gbit/sec 4G up to 1 Gbit/sec, average 14 Mbit/sec (MIMO 42 Mbit/sec) 3G UHF 850MHz–1900MHz min 200 kbit/sec (approx 0.2 Mbit/sec)
	Cell, Femtocell, GSM, CDMA2000, TD-SCDMA, WiMAX, LTE

(continued)

TABLE i.2   Continued

Wifi WLAN	IEEE 802.11a, b, g, n, 2012, ac, ad Web pages: SSL Encrypted: WEP, WPA, WPA2, WPS 2.4GHz UHF and 5GHz SHF radio waves
Fibre optics	1200 to nanometer wavelengths 1680 e.g. 2.56 Tb/sec 25 Gb/sec to 270 Gb/sec per channel 1 Petabit/sec up to 100 Petabits/sec 500MHz–1000MHz 850–1550nm wavelengths
Bluetooth	v1.0, 1.2, 2.0. 2,1, 3.0 v4.0 Bluetooth low energy UHF ISM band from 2.4GHz–2.485GHz
NFC (Near-field communication)	based on RFID ISO/IEC 14443 and FeliCa
Proximity, smart card	ISO/IEC 14443 Comms protocol ISO/IEC 15693 vicinity Card, ISO/IEC 6523 , 15459 Registration
RFID	RF bands, LF, HF, UHF, Microwave (1GHz–100GHz)
GPS satellite	1575.42MHz (L1) and 1227.60MHz (L2)
Commercial radio	FM, MW, LW, SW, satellite, DAB (digital radio) channels
Commercial television	UHF, digital, satellite
Aircraft traffic, taxis, medical bands, emergency service bands	UHF, VHF, digital encrypted
NMEA 0183, 2000 echo sounder, sonars	100Hz–500Hz 160–235Db
Anemometers (wind), gyrocompass, autopilot	
Voice frequency	Audio sound 20Hz–20,000Hz

Identification of the type of network topology and the range of device protocol spectrum is very much part of the digital enterprise story. At a personal level, mobile devices using near field communication (NFC) proximity technology enable new contactless services such as financial payments in shops or connections to wearable exercise devices. Taking a wider perspective, mobile cell phone coverage, satellite navigation, and Wi-Fi hotspots enable connectivity while traveling on roads, rail, and abroad, whether in cars, trains, aircraft, or ships. At economy and market level, city-wide municipal networks enable transport and emergency services, and also expedite new initiatives, such as open data services that provide community information and local business services support. With telecommunication networks spanning global time zones and enterprise data centers, these changes are driving the digital economy. Borders between countries and industry models are being torn down by the digital continuum and the tiers of internetworking infrastructure.

New Architecture Practices for the Digital World

The connection between infrastructure networks and the devices and objects that work to enable human/machine intermediation shapes how digital technologies can service and enable the digital enterprise value network.

There are a number of emerging digital-oriented enterprise architectural themes that represent a new kind of thinking and pragmatism which affects companies and individuals, start-ups, multinationals, and major cities. These digital era architecture practices include:

- Commodity, core, and transformational thinking
- Prototyping and agility
- Empathy and aesthetics
- Immersive sensing and feedback
- Geospatial and stereoscopic augmentation
- Modularity and disruption
- Design thinking
- Generativity and monetization
- Platforms.

Commodity, core, and transformational thinking

Legacy systems can be a burden for the future, and may need modernization or replacement. C-level executives regularly have to deal with this issue, in which decisions and investments have to be prioritized. Questions continually arise when new technology is introduced, and re-engineering the business model through consolidation and rationalization or through mergers and acquisition is a critical issue for business transformation.

This all affects the capabilities of the enterprise, and collectively defines the portfolio of capabilities of the enterprise operating model. A foundational principle that applies to this kind of strategic portfolio management thinking is the ability to focus on what is important from a risk and mission imperative perspective. In the case studies, we explore this practice, identifying strategic capabilities that define process, systems, and resources. Digital technologies influence how these capabilities are developed by strategic leadership and in particular how enterprise strategy and performance are shaped. Identifying the vision and direction of the enterprise is not separate from digital strategy but an integral part of the whole strategy.

Programmatic planning of IT infrastructure and applications costs is a widespread practice in both large and small organizations. In many industries that are technology intensive, such as financial services and IT services, the average IT operational budget is 3.6 percent of company turnover, ranging from 2.9 percent to 6 percent.[17] This figure varies by geographic region and may change as the move from capital- to subscription-based services becomes more common, thanks to cloud computing technology. It is not untypical to see thousands of employees and thousands of applications and interfaces hosted across multiple data centers in large multinational companies. Prioritizing the IT budget spend on essential IT services over general administration and productivity tools makes a difference in the legacy rationalization of day-to-day IT costs. What is more important, however, is that the impact of digital technology to change business outcomes is potentially more significant. Social media impact on customer experience, data analytics driving enhanced decisions, and the rise of mobile devices to empower employees and customers is raised to a new level of IT budget prioritization of what is commodity- and core-essential, and mission transformational.

Prototyping and agility

A second key feature of digital technologies is the rise of rapid design, sourcing, and visualization. New digital prototyping methodologies that seek to increase the immersion and high-quality user experience (UX) of the design process is increasingly key to the successful design of customer experience (CX). This is not new in systems engineering practices, but thanks to the rapid visualization that is possible with many user experience and website tools that are based on an on-demand cloud computing environment, it is increasingly a participatory feature. A number of the case studies show significant use of the agile method to establish rapid development and direct engagement with customers and employees, in order to transform both new and existing digital enterprise capabilities.

Prototyping is now a key feature in development platforms and services for web applications and mobile applications. Technologies from software and services providers such as ADITI, BlinkMobile, Globo, MyOxygen, and many others provide UX and CX design and integration to blend company data content with products and services through smartphones and tablets. A major feature of these platforms is the ability to prototype mobile application solutions in hours rather than days or weeks from concept to publishing and use. Mobile Applications Management (MAM) and Mobile Device Management (MDM) are now strategic platform priorities for many major enterprises in their efforts to build agility into their websites and mobile channels, in order to reach more customers and citizens. These digital technology management platforms are often essential to enable connection to device-neutral services such as BYOD (bring your own device). They also provide a better-integrated user experience of managed content to and from mobile devices. From the perspective of the end user, these digital technologies have a direct and tangible impact on operational working practices. For example, in retail it is common practice now to develop front-end mobile applications that empower store employees to connect to the back office stock and planning systems, so they can place and track replenishment orders for stock items, through scanning barcodes in store.

Empathy and aesthetics

A third important plank of digital thinking is the change in human experience and its "immersive" quality through aesthetics and empathy that are influenced by digitization. The visual artistry of providing information that engages the senses is central to high-quality digital design. In discussions with practitioners in the entertainment theater and arts world in particular, it has become clear that the ability to use digital technologies to engage audiences in "live" experiences is a powerful and compelling feature of the digital world. It is not just the wow factor of visuals on a mobile device or an interactive public display board that promote events and products, but it is how human activities and working spaces integrate in a synergistic way to maximize the potential experience.

Giving visualization more impact for the user is increasingly essential to mobile touchscreen interaction and on-screen alerts. Perhaps an extreme example is the online gaming industry, which has made considerable advances in the use of high-end multi-core and multi-tread graphics processors to create ever more intensive visuals and gaming experiences. This is a significant market, as Intel recently indicated at their annual Developers Conference in San Francisco. In the public keynote speeches, Kirk Skaugen, SVP & General Manager of PV Client Group, stated that "There are 711 million PC gamers on the planet today, that's about 1 in 10 people are gamers, it's a key statistic and a huge market opportunity."[18]

Immersive sensing and feedback

A fourth feature of digitization is the rise of embedded sensors and sensor networks that enable responsive feedback. The spread of Wi-Fi and other network technologies enables connections to mobile devices, embedded sensors, and other smart objects in the places in which we live and work. Knowing how to use these technologies is key to building a digital enterprise that is truly connected to the environment and the value network. A number of case studies show practitioners seeking ways in which to collect information and build sensing environments for their customers, suppliers, and employees.

An example of immersive feedback is haptic design in mobile devices. This is the sense of touch and feel from the device as part of the user experience. Simple vibration is one example, but this will become more sophisticated with the continuing development of wearable devices: these can stimulate the skin to alert users passively or actively, simply by using vibration. As an example, haptic specialist hack has created a vibrating timekeeper that vibrates at different frequencies to signal the passing of time.[19, 20] *The concept of immersive feedback is not limited to touch and feel, but also encompasses augmentation and enhancement of the live space with digital technologies. This idea is particularly strong in performing arts and theaters where light, sound, and digital technologies can create a much greater sense of action and audience participation. Although common practice in the world's theme parks, of course, this vision is now moving to other enterprises, with embedded sensors and feedback augmenting user experience.*

Geospatial and stereoscopic augmentation

The fifth key feature of digitization has been its ubiquitous spread across spatial boundaries. The advent of digital mapping has created a completely new industry of online maps and satellite navigation, and this has empowered a new generation of spatial services. Google maps, bing, Apple, and many others have made this technology available in mobile devices to provide images and street-level accuracy to travel directions and location services. But it has not stopped there: buildings and rooms have been mapped, and devices such as Apple's iBeacon™ is an indoor proximity system that enables Bluetooth low-energy proximity sensing to transmit identifiers to determine locations within a room.[21] It also supports detections of mobile device presence to trigger check-ins on social media or push notifications automatically to the mobile user, based on preferences. The ability to create digital spatial mapping has gone to ever finer levels, which is continuing evolve: 3D scanning technology now enables physical objects such as furniture to be digitized into a virtual model, which connects and stores location data at an unprecedented level of detail. New technology like this is changing how we think about physical spaces and the way we interact with objects and services within them. This is a key challenge and an exciting opportunity in the building of digital workspaces.

An example of geospatial thinking can be seen in the healthcare industry, where geo-fencing technology enables patients fitted with wearable GPS location tagging to be monitored to ensure they are protected and kept from harm. In the consumer market, rapid advances in 3D scanning are coming to consumer mobiles and tablets. Intel Context cameras are an example of immersive scanning technology that can map context location information. This technology, called Intel RealSense™,²² is embedded in a tablet or a mobile with a scanner that can take a 3D image of an object and, with stereoscopic algorithms, compute its real-world physical dimensions. This can be uploaded into a context cloud database and used in virtual models of the physical environment. Apple recently acquired the Primesense 3D tech company and the itSee3D™ scanning technology that generates image data in 3D.²³ The spatial design of physical workspaces is now enabled by digital space mapping, which in the near future will be part of everyday living spaces.

Modularity and disruption

The sixth key feature of digitization has been the ability to take IT that has been turned into "containered services" and treat these services as modular, scalable building blocks. The evolution of digital technologies has seen a convergence of standards and technological advances in computing, software, and miniaturization as well as a massive scaling out of networks and infrastructure resources. Cloud computing has led the establishment of a catalog and marketplace context so that today we see large digital component markets such as the Android market, iOS market, API markets, and many other scalable architecture resources available on demand. Digitization has both commoditized and componentized these cloud-oriented architectures as well as placing the computation power in the palms of our hands, with mobile smart devices that 30 years ago would have been equivalent to a supercomputer. Architecture has become modular in the sense that it can be constructed from building blocks of content – both software and hardware. Disruption in the market comes through the fact that digital technologies are able to advance to market faster because modular adoption and digital platforms enable quick and pervasive adoption, as users access services and use powerful devices to get work done. A number of case studies show practitioners in the field of embedded technologies seeking ways in which to integrate digital technologies with the supply chain, to enable efficiency and new digital business models.

Examples of modularity and disruption have perhaps been most visible in the consumer world with the impact of the Apple iPod and iPhone on the music and mobile device industry. Several disruptive changes are well documented in the shift to downloadable and streaming music, which has fundamentally changed the way in which customers consume music. The iPhone's introduction in 2007 was a disruptive step change, with its combination of touchscreen, mobile applications, and radical new form disrupting the old world of single-purpose communication devices. The new smartphone market is by all measures booming, with unit sales from all the top vendors growing by over 40 percent, revenue up by 20 percent, and profits up by 50 percent.[24] Modularity in the architecture of these devices has been a key part of this growth. The software, the content, and applications are all "plug-and-play," enabling a new kind of rapid scalability not seen previously. The mobile device itself is a modular platform, with yearly or even quarterly incremental enhancements, which are followed by step changes that include new architecture such as the iPad and connected wearables.

Design thinking

A seventh consequence of these new architecture principles has been the impact on philosophy and creativity through the use of digital in the design process. "Design thinking" is defined as cognitive activities that designers apply during the process of designing.[25] It is the combination of empathy for the context of the problem, the creativity to generate ideas and insights, and the rationality to analyze and generate solutions to the problem. According to Tim Brown, CEO and president of IDEO, the goal of design thinking is "matching people's needs with what is technologically feasible and viable as a business strategy."[26] This is critically important in digital technologies that are linked intimately with the business and social outcomes they influence and create. Design thinking uses a scientific approach to creativity and rational design. It is not just thinking about architecture design from the building blocks but creating scenarios that drive solutions to meet the desired outcomes. The conceptualization of design philosophy is changing through digitization. Deliberately planned design is giving way to a more fluid modeling approach that may test many possible solutions before moving to a chosen design. Design outcome trajectories may be tested more rapidly and with greater repeatability, as new generations of simulation and design tools enable rapid analysis of design outcomes. The concept of modularity is used to create rapid incremental services and capability advances, and then step-change jumps. New kinds of architectural design styles are emerging as practitioners seek new ways in which to "break institutional thinking" and move more rapidly toward new digital adoption capabilities.

Examples of design thinking are evident in the disruptive example of cell phone design we observed in the previous section on modularity. Other examples can be seen with Intel and its research and development into ever faster computing chip design. Intel is still pushing this, but their former chief architect, Bob Colwell, suggests that Moore's law is "headed for a cliff." According to Colwell, the maximum extension of the law, in which transistor densities continue doubling every 18 to 24 months, will be hit in 2020 or 2022, around 7nm or 5nm.[27] Yet Intel is already using design thinking to move round this barrier with multi-core and multi-thread technology, and the evolution of other forms of technology such as quantum computing. In the everyday world, design thinking is becoming a feature where large-scale data and social networks challenge traditional market and organizational thinking. New business models that crowdsource testing and development to software distribution marketplaces are challenging how work can be done to solve business problems.

Generativity and monetization

An eighth architecturally enabled phenomenon has been effective mass scaling through mass adoption of digitization in products and services. The so-called "viral effect" describes much of the underpinning change in potential that has brought faster growth and quicker digital services. Digital technology drives new kinds of consumer adoption cycles. Consumer behavior in social networks, especially instant feedback, can drive a viral self-reinforcement that has the potential to scale user adoption rapidly.

Monetization of the digital enterprise can exploit this by using digital technologies to create advantage and value. In the case studies we seek to understand the relationship between market outcomes and customer experience, which is driven by digital enterprise capabilities. The case studies show how different monetization mechanisms drive value to consumers and build the performance of the digital enterprise.

Examples of the generative scaling of moneymaking opportunities on the internet are manifold in the popular press. A recent high-profile example in the gaming industry is the acquisition of Twitch, the online gaming spectator portal, by Amazon. Twitch hit one million active monthly broadcasters in January 2014.[28] As Emmett Shear, the CEO, said in his open letter on accepting the Amazon bid, "It's almost unbelievable that slightly more than 3 years ago, Twitch didn't exist."[29] The ability to generate scalable social communities is a powerful phenomenon of digital technologies, which in the right circumstances can grow to huge numbers and high value. Yet it is not just increasing audiences that create the power of digital generativity; it is also the access to resources and services that support and enable enterprise processes. An early example of this took place in 2008, when Amazon entered the cloud computing business,[30] using cheap cloud computing resources. This service was used by the New York Times to rapidly process 150 years of newspaper articles into an online archive. The data-intensive goal was to convert 11 million articles published from the founding of the newspaper in 1851 until 1989, so that they were available through its website search engine. The New York Times scanned in the stories, cut up into columns to fit the scanners (as TIFF files), then uploaded them to the Amazon Cloud Storage S3™ platform. Then, using Amazon's EC2™ computing platform, they ran a PDF conversion app that converted the 4TB of TIFF data into 1.5TB of PDF files. Using 100 Linux computers, the job took about 24 hours. Today this is commonplace, with ever-increasing speed and performance, and is a core part of using digital technologies.

Platforms

The final key design feature of digitization has been the creation of "digital platforming," where digital technologies act as an enabler for "market makers," bringing together products, services, customers, and suppliers. It has been said by some industry observers that we are living in a "subscription economy" and a "sharing economy." This means that assets are no longer owned but rented and consumed as you go, and a recurring revenue metrics model exists for consumers and providers. By sharing assets in an incremental manner, consumers can choose from a wider variety of products and services, while providers and partners can access a potentially larger market. Digitization can allow consumers to access products and services that are less constrained by physical location or ownership. Economically it may not be right for all scenarios, but it illustrates a more fundamental aspect of digital technologies, which is the emergence of *platforms*. Underpinning digital services, whether on a mobile device, a tablet, a website, or in an automobile or a building, a digital platform is usually a constructed environment that enables the digital content, services, and experience to be engineered and managed for quality outcomes. It does not happen by magic, but when the design experience and the usability of the digital service become entangled and an immersive experience, it feels seamless and frictionless – almost magical.

Examples of platforms in the digital economy can be found in many business to business (B2B) and business to consumer (B2C) industries. Large-scale B2B marketplaces occur in many industries, from pharmaceuticals to the automotive supply chain. TradeB2B.com, canbiotch.com, and worldbidpharmaceutical.com are examples of biotechnology and pharmaceuticals portals, and B2B marketplaces in a heavily regulated and segmented industry. Non-prescription, prescription, B2B wholesale, government-level pharma, the active pharmaceutical ingredients market, and the R&D market are some of the many segments. Allautowares.com is a global B2B web portal for the automotive industry; and S-Gate is the global BMW Group dealer and importer portal. There are many other examples throughout the supply chain. In the consumer industry, B2C is emerging everywhere. Examples include liazon.com, which acts as a portal for employee health services, saving time and money for employees and employers in finding the right health package. OpenTable.com is a ubiquitous source of reservations that creates a community of feedback that is based on likes and dislikes of restaurants and dining experiences.[31] *New crowdsourcing models have created a "sharing economy" that is enabled by new digital platforms. Examples include Sourceforge.com for Open Source software; Wikipedia.com as a collaborative internet encyclopedia; Piratebay.com for peer-to-peer (P2P) file sharing; Kiva for P2P finance; and Neighborgoods.com for collaborative consumption.[32] Platforms are a core feature of digital technologies and the building of digital enterprises and digital market economies.*

Introduction Summary

In the Introduction we have examined the technological revolution that is unfolding in the physical and digital economies. The advent of new thinking is clear, with data, processes, and social interactions being transformed by digitization. A key aim of this book is to explore the impact of these trends and to establish examples of practice found in today's enterprises. Chapter 1 will lay the foundations for the trends in technology that are driving these changes, and will start to describe the changes in architecture and platforms that are emerging.

part I

Architecture in the Era of Digital Ecosystems

Trends of Technological Ecosystems

Chapter Introduction

The pervasive adoption of digital technologies across all industries is a global phenomenon. Materially, the internet economy, which represents online transactional data, may only represent 10 percent of the Gross Domestic Product of countries but per annum this is growing at 8 to 10 percent, far outpacing growth in traditional physical "bricks and mortar" sectors defined as physical goods and services that are traded off-internet.[1] Viewing internet transactions is only part of the wider evolution of how human activity is using digital technology in all manner of social and business activity. Technology frequently enables activities in an augmented way, adding more value to telephone conversations, email, searching for information, or completing a document, taking a photograph, or listening to music. There is a greater than tenfold growth forecast in the next decade for mobile and data traffic alone, and there is a commensurate forecast in the rise of the "Internet of Things." Technological ecosystems are emerging that are becoming fused into the very fabric of society and economies, and these are creating network effects that pervade the digital economy. Online presence through websites and, increasingly, mobile devices has become highly interconnected, forming *ecosystems* of association and technologies. This interconnected effect has enabled value creation through what some describe as "multi-sided platform" (MSP) business models. Groups of people, enterprises, and markets are able to meet and trade, share and collaborate through digital technologies that generate new social and business monetization models.[2]

In this chapter, we will explore the definition of this clustering effect, be it related to people, products, or services that are using technologies, and what this may mean for the future of economic and enterprise development.

We will cover the following topics:

- Digital economy and ecosystems
- Definition of the digital ecosystem
- Definition of vertical and horizontal digital ecosystems
- Definition of the digital enterprise
- The rise of technological ecosystems
- Introduction to digital technologies
- The state of digital technology and enterprise.

The Connected Enterprise

To illustrate practitioner perspectives, let us look at two examples of the value network ecosystem that exist in two industries: the smart hotel ecosystem and the connected car ecosystem.

"Smart hotel" digital ecosystem

In the digital world, with virtual communities of customers and potential consumers, the evolution of vertical and horizontal value is a key concept for building a digital enterprise. In the example of the hotel and leisure industry, we can clearly see how physical meeting places and digital ecosystems are converging. Vertical and horizontal digital ecosystems are influencing the design of the digital enterprise.

The hotel room is a "physical workplace object" that can have many connected spaces. Corporate and social events may be managed in the same premises, requiring different utilization of rooms and facilities. Customer services, whether the service desk, concierge services, room service and housekeeping, or building maintenance, are all facets of service enablement. Then there are the services at work in the rooms, such as TV remotes, TV entertainment, room service calls, cleaning services, and in-room dining. A gymnasium and other facilities create additional capabilities that all provide additional value for the customer experience and increase monetization opportunities for the business.

The "smart hotel" will have many points of contact with the customer, from face to face to virtually, via digital technology, and therefore many opportunities to build brand loyalty and engage customers in order to offer new value experience. This contact can be before, during, and after a visit and via the hotel and its partners. It is an ecosystem of value networks that spreads across customers, hotels, their employees, and partners. Each network is a combination of vertical integration (such as the ordering and reordering of food and beverages from suppliers to the consumption of these items) and horizontal integration (across different locations, to provide consistent customer experience and efficient operations). These MSP platforms will enable customer loyalty systems as well as cross-selling to flight, food, and business services that expand the scope and potential value for the customers and the hotel. The digital enterprise for a "smart hotel" is much more than its physical room and assets; it is how each customer experiences the augmentation of grounds, foyer, rooms, and all the services before, during, and after the visit to the hotel. All these elements become the total service.

"Connected automobile" digital ecosystem

While a hotel is an example of a connected physical space, the value network ecosystem also applies to moving objects as well. A good example of this is the connected car, which is seeking to automate and enhance every aspect of the vehicle's lifecycle, from concept design to manufacture, sales to aftermarket operation, and the customer driving experience. This is not limited to inside the vehicle but also relates to traffic networks and to other vehicles' ecosystems.

This mindset connects the digitally enabled car to the logistics supply chain as a total lifecycle concept. A range of embedded technologies have been created that include Advanced Vehicle Driver Assistance (ADAS) technologies for safety and sustainable energy management. Vehicle to Vehicle (V2V) provides in-transit management of other vehicles and objects relative to the vehicle and driver. Car infotainment provides remote content delivery and personalization for driver and passengers, which links with mobile devices and applications. Pre-planning trips or selected and downloading movies, music, and games can all be done remotely in synchronization with the on-board systems. Remote diagnostics, spare parts reordering, and planned maintenance can all be automated, with remote downloading and monitoring of vehicle health and performance. Virtual reality car showrooms, in-car head-up display controls for line-of-sight information, and self-driving cars are all possible today. The connected automotive ecosystem touches many associated objects and the customer driving experience inside and outside the car. It is this extended and connected system of systems that is the digital enterprise of the future.

The vertical and horizontal value chains are being impacted by digital platforms that enable new value network ecosystems to be constructed throughout a business model. Whether you are looking at how to engage your customers in your products and services, seeking how to collect the right analytical data to gain insight into better informed decisions and judgments or user experiences, or seeking ways to build better B2B and B2C collaboration, digital technologies are reshaping how we can archi- tect these workspaces and the enterprise.

At the heart of these examples is the impact of digital enterprise on industries and their associated physical and digital interconnectedness.

Digital enterprise

A form of organizational structure with a legal basis, enabled by technologies to provide physical or virtual products or services in one or more digital ecosystems. The organization physically and virtually operates monetization mechanisms that generate social and financial value in one or more digital economies.

Ultimately, the goal is to collaborate and to scale according to demand and supply, thereby meeting the constituent members' needs. These can evolve as communities and relations form, coalesce, and dissipate, which is referred to as *co-presence*. The value creation process is centered around how the digital enterprise enables these experiences to generate co-benefits and worth, as defined by monetary and other social value for all parties. A definition of a digital enterprise perhaps encompasses all these things.

The Rise of Technological Ecosystems

Understanding how technology creates digital ecosystems is an important place to start in building a digital enterprise. The term "digital," as stated in the previous section, is a catch-all term used to define many types of technological viewpoints that exist today.

In the next section, we will explore the types of emerging clusters of technologies that define the viewpoints of digital ecosystems and how they are part of building digital enterprises. It is particularly useful given the perceptions and bias that can easily set in when describing the internet as an "ecosystem" with a set of devices, networks, and web services. Whilst the internet is the largest man-made "system" on the planet in terms of geographic scale, without a doubt, it is not the only technology that makes up the smorgasbord of innovations and inventions that are available to technologists and business practitioners. I will examine seven such clusters, but by no means are these the only ones. By definition, ecosystems will continually evolve new topologies and capabilities over time, thereby generating new ecosystems.

The seven technological ecosystems viewpoints we will explore are:

- Information ecosystems
- Supply chain technology network ecosystems
- Advanced technology engineering transformation ecosystems
- Technology in the workplace ecosystems
- Open and propriety platforms ecosystems
- Enterprise vendor technologies ecosystems
- Privacy, confidentiality, security, and trust ecosystems.

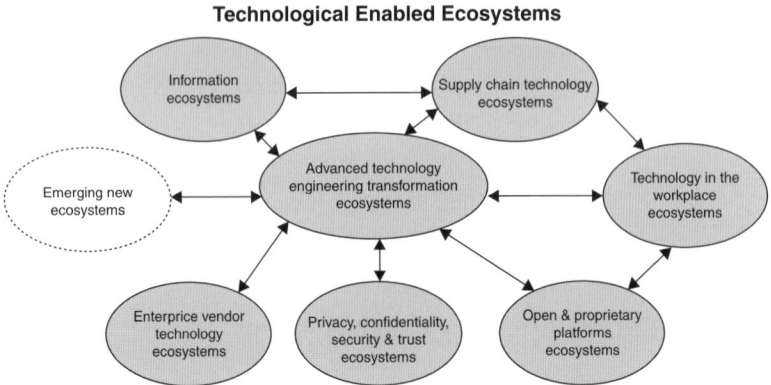

FIGURE 1.1 Examples of technological ecosystems viewpoints

Technology Ecosystem Viewpoint 1: The Information Ecosystems

The growth of information on the internet has reached staggering proportions, and is accelerating. To estimate the number of web pages and the number of links that connect those pages is difficult, but there were over 1 billion websites in September 2014.[3] According to Verisign's latest Domain Name Industry Brief, more than 6 million domain names were registered in the last quarter of 2012, bringing the total to 252 million worldwide.[4]

The power of this collective digitization of information is an ecosystem that potentially spans every conceivable information domain and physical location. This is the first technological ecosystem with a completely pervasive impact. Access and search engine capabilities will vary depending on the region of the world you live in, but the potential for digital information is clear.

The semantic web is an idea developed by the World Wide Web Consortium (W3C), an international standards body, which has developed a number of ideas and standards in this area.[5]

The concepts of Web 1.0, Web 2.0, Web 3.0, and Web 4.0 have grown in recent years to define this information ecosystem perspective.

- Web 1.0 – static information on web pages
- Web 2.0 – user-generated dynamic data and social media growth[6]
- Web 3.0 – information both structured and unstructured is identified semantically and put into a common framework that allows data to be shared and reused across application, enterprise, and community boundaries: "a web of data that can be processed by machines"[7]
- Web 4.0 – the intelligent web, which uses machine learning and cognitive intelligence to create interactive human and machine systems.[8]

We are currently at the stage of Web 2.0, and emerging technologies are starting to form Web 3.0 and Web 4.0 ontologies.

An information domain is a cluster of information classified by the information archetype about itself and its related features.

Physical domains have features and information that relate to that physical domain. These can be clustered to form information archetypes about the domains.

Search engines, queries, and all manner of different data analytics are made possible by analyzing this raw material, together with its associated relationships and behaviors. Table 1.1 is a sample of the enormous range of information that can inhabit the information ecosystem.

The key is in understanding the relationships between the information domains and the physical domains. They create spaces of information in context. As in Figure 1.1, the movement toward Web 3.0 and Web 4.0 is the construction of meaningful workspaces that enable machines and humans to gain semantic information and move toward intelligent augmented experience.

Technology Ecosystem Viewpoint 2: Technology in the Supply Chain Network

The concept of the supply chain has been around for years: it was probably one of the foundations of the industrial revolution and latterly the

34

TABLE 1.1 Examples of information and physical domain ecosystem mappings

Information Domains			Physical Domains		
Archetype	Key search goals	Key information features	Archetype	Key search goals	Key information features
Economic Commercial	Growth Stability Continuity Equity	• Macro economics • Micro economics • Socio-economics • Metrics, qualities • Value, value systems • Contracts • Intellectual property • Monetization	**Geographic Domains, Dominions**	Market segments Skills & resources	• Legal, political, ethics • CSR, governance, policies, social behaviors, preferences
Sourcing	Capabilities Competencies Density Co-presence	• Managed hosting • Single sourcing • Multisourcing • Co-sourcing • Crowdsourcing	**Processes, Conversions, Transformations**	Context awareness and optimization loops Automation	• Internet of Things, pervasive computing enterprise systems • Industrialization
Acquisition	Manipulation Analysis Trading	• Orchestration • Aggregation • Broker reseller	**Systems Domains**		
Integration		• Isolation • Encapsulation • Federation	**Organizational Structures**	Workplaces, user experiences	
Connectivity	Specification architecture	• Distribution • Replication • Exposure	**People**		• Workflow • Platforms • Manufacturing – 3D • Marketplaces • Services • Digitalization of work practices

Internetworking	Interfaces Entanglement Multiplexity Multiplicity	• Network topologies • Domains • Appliances • Interfaces	**Avatars, Agents, Virtual People** Social, KM, mashups, augmentation, VR, contextual awareness	• Communities • Virtual teams • Virtual organizations • Virtual businesses • Virtual services
Code	Digitization Creation	• Content • Versions, configuration • Operating systems • Frameworks • Languages • SDKs, IDEs	**Data, Metadata** Services, data, objects, knowledge, sensing, metadata	• Groups • Collectives • Individuality • Self-interest/bias • Rights
Security, Privacy	Ownership Protection Containment	• Identity • Encryption • Authorization • Cyber threat • DR, BC	**Devices & Sensors** Mobile comms, wearables, fixed, mobile embedded biometrics, ML, voice, AI, cognition	• Mobile comms • Wearables • Fixed, Mobile • Embedded • Biometrics • ML • Voice • AI • Cognition

modern industrial economy. Business processes were separated and managed across a complex of operations that enabled access to markets and labor as well as economies of scale. This general principle was based on the notion of physical separation of tasks, and labor could be managed and distributed through a chain of supply to meet market demand. Yet this idea has been radically altered with the advent of global telecommunications networks and the internet-based virtual processes on top. Many traditional supply chains have opened up into virtual organizations (VOs) that either in whole or in part can function equally if not better through online channels. The supply chain becomes the supply network ecosystem of processes, which presents new opportunities and challenges that thereby allow enterprises to rethink their business model.

There have been three major transformational shifts that have resulted in a technology ecosystem surrounding the supply chain:

1. **Physical supply chain network**, which represents the physicality of the supply chain.
2. **E-commerce models**, which represent how monetary transactions are conducted.
3. **Virtual supply chain network**, which is the structure brought about by digitization of the physical supply chain and e-commerce models, creating virtual supply chain business processes and digital value network models.

The digital supply chain can be considered as being made up of these three concepts. The physical supply chain, digitized by new information technologies, enables e-commerce models that in turn enable new digital supply chain business processes and a virtual supply chain.

Firstly, a major change caused by the digital technologies has been the creation of e-commerce models that can enable the potential in any business process to be monetized and charged through an online transactional model. This perspective has been described by the B2B, B2C, and latterly new collaborative models that use crowdsourcing (social networking and collaboration) to generate a Consumer to Consumer (C2C) model.

Secondly, the movement of physical asset ownership to a subscription or "pay-as-you-go"-based economic model has driven opportunities for a leaner supply chain operation. This is achieved by exploiting supply chain partners who may host part of the business supply chain, rather than the enterprise investing in its own assets. The overall effect is a shift from a physical supply chain to a more modular virtual supply chain network operation, which has new performance potential.

Thirdly, the design of the business model is altered through the use of digital technologies, which can extend the reach of sourcing and net-working to customers through one or multiple channels to market. These are not limited to physical contact but include mobile smart devices and web marketplaces, enabling what in computing language is described as *multiplexing* and *multiplicity* of services. This means that more products and services can be offered to customers online, creating a wider set of options and a broader market to sell to and service. The challenge in building the digital enterprise is in defining the business processes and business models that can be realized through these digital technologies. Examples of this transformation shift in physical to virtual supply chain can be seen across industries, many examples are illustrated in Table 1.2.

TABLE 1.2   Examples of physical to virtual supply chain processes

Physical Business Process	Virtual Business Process
Sourcing	• Multi-source, co-source, crowdsource • Outsourcing and offshore • Marketplaces, partnerships, and alliances
Design	• Collaborative design, virtual design • Simulation • Technology refresh, quantum disruption • Metrics and quality
Manufacturing	• Trials, to stock, to order • Additive manufacture • Robotics, federated
Service and Aftercare	• Auto-response to service request • Service assist and self-service • Service augmentation – contextualization

(continued)

TABLE 1.2 Continued

Transport and Logistics	• Intelligent transport networks • Shared/co-location
Warehousing and Distribution	• Auto-response • Service assist • Service augmentation – contextualization • Crowdshipping
Assembly	• Robotic assembly • Integrated material supply • Dynamic planning & control
Maintenance and Diagnostic	• Smart spares and component embedded diagnostics and geo-reporting • Auto-lifecycle replenish management • Research to field integration (translation)
Fuel, Materials	• Smart meters • Alternative, reusable fuels • Sustainable materials • Smart materials, solar panels
Compliance and Policy	• Tracking and traceability • Intelligent resource management • Smart buildings
Sales and Marketing	• Gamification • Dynamic pricing • Behavior analytics
Human Capital Management	• Crowdsourcing knowledge management • Offshore, near, onshore • Multi-skilling
Social Business Models	• Consumer behavior analytics/gamification • Augmented product/services
Crowd Network Models	• Open innovation, multi-process • Crowd funding • Virtual markets, B2B, C2B, G2B
Social Technical Models	• Internet of Things – embedded technology networks • Simulation, computer design, manufacture
Research and Development	• Translation research • Ideation incubators • Agile to market development

Technology Ecosystem Viewpoint 3: Advanced Technology Transformation Engineering

While the information revolution and the supply chain have seen changes through digitization, in parallel there has been continual creativity and innovation in technology. Often it is these conjunctions that have introduced new ideas that in the right circumstances have moved from incremental change to disruptive technology, which is capable of redefining whole markets and creating new products and services.

Digitization has the ability to change the nature of what is recorded, the speed of information, and how information and experience is processed. We will explore these themes in later chapters, but as an introduction it is important to put this type of technological ecosystem into perspective. In our first diagram of technological ecosystems, Figure 1.1, advanced technology engineering transformation is at the center connecting to all other technology ecosystems: the reason for this is that technological innovation can impact all ecosystems (see Figure 1.2).

To illustrate this point, consider how technological innovation such as web telepresence or 3D printing can change existing methods. One has the ability to connect us in real time and to communicate over wireless or mobile systems to share video images and the sounds of places and people that could be thousands of miles away. The other has enabled digital data that defines a virtual object to be entered into a 3D printer to generate a physical object facsimile of the digital representation. Again, this can be done potentially in any location, with the printer either on the ground or even in an orbiting space station, as long as there are the right raw materials and communication protocols to understand the digital data model. What is happening in the first case is that the moment of time, the temporality, is being altered from the physical minutes, hours, or days it would have taken for a person to have the experience in real time. The spatial awareness and locality have also shifted from the physical to the virtual, as digital technologies can compress large-scale information about objects and spaces and recreate these digitally. The concept of "what is real?" is introduced, in that objects and experiences can be both physical and virtual (see Figure 1.3).

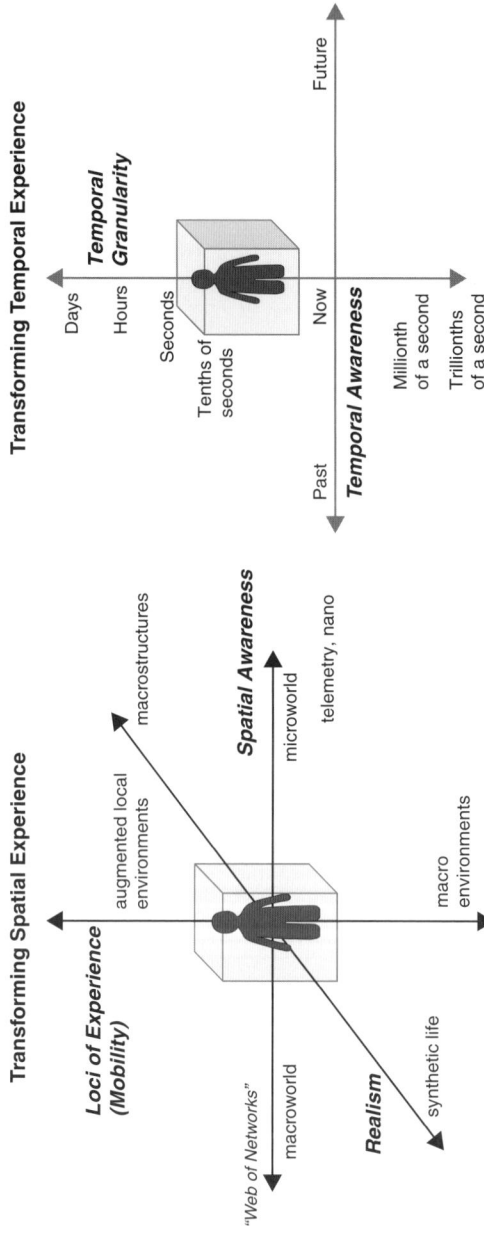

FIGURE 1.2 The shift of time and space by advanced technology engineering transformations

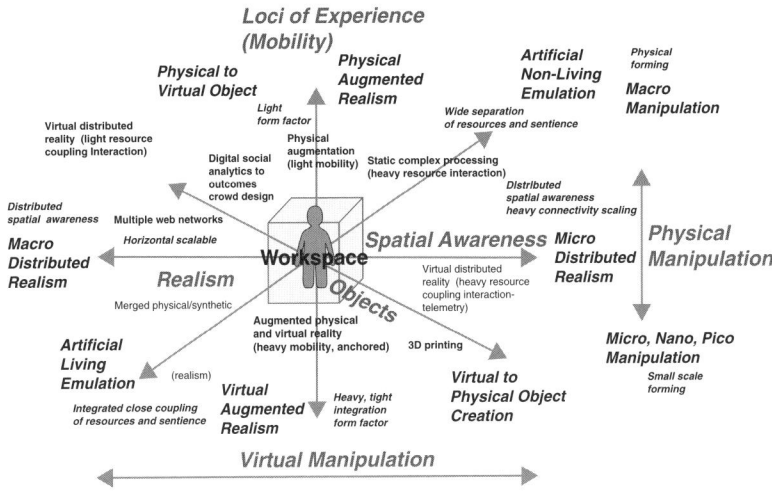

FIGURE 1.3 Advanced technology transformations changing workspace capabilities

TABLE 1.3 Advanced technology engineering transformation

Advanced Technology Engineering Transformations	Examples of Advanced Technologies
Spatial awareness – macro-distributed realism	Virtual digital maps
Spatial awareness – micro distributed realism	Large-scale sensors networks, for example, earthquake early warning systems
Loci of experience – physical augmented realism	Virtual reality augmentation
Loci of experience - virtual augmented realism	Virtual (gaming) world such as Second Life or digital mall
Physical to virtual objects creation	Digital social analytics to outcomes, crowd design
Virtual to physical objects creation	3D printing
Artificial non-living emulation	Simulation and complex object analysis, examples include 3D engineering design and biomolecular engineering and genetic simulation
Artificial living emulation	Synthetic avatars, voice emulation, artificial intelligence
Macro manipulation – meters, tens of meters, kilometers	Robotics, mega earth movers, deep space communications and controls
Micro manipulation – micro, nano, pico scale	Wearable tech, nano tech, genetic engineering

There are many such examples that illustrate changes in the way digital information is used and perceived. They represent a frontier of what is possible and, importantly, a way of rethinking and reimagining the boundaries of what is and might be possible. By its very nature it creates new kinds of technologically enabled ecosystems (see Table 1.3). Consider these few game-changing examples.

Technology Ecosystem Viewpoint 4: Open and Proprietary Technology and Platforms

Previous technological ecosystems have been primarily based on physical properties of technologies to transform how humans and machines work and computation gets done. These factors can be managed commercially through the technology standards that are placed in them for code, messages, and protocols that are used to describe and share these capabilities. A fourth important type of technological ecosystem is based on how these standards of openness and connected communities exist. Probably the three key areas that have emerged to define this type of technological ecosystem are:

- **Open technical architecture standards** that support a range of services that may be from third parties as well as the original equipment owner.
- **Embedded technologies**, which encode digital content and functionality into the physical objects.
- **Interoperability and portability standards**, which enable different brands and technology standards used in products and services to collaborate and work together where enabled.

Firstly, the development of open standards for the internet and mobile and wireless networks has been the foundation for a global connected infrastructure. HTTP, XML, URL, 3G, 4G, and others have enabled the technical sharing of content and services that hitherto would have been impossible without common standards for sharing data. On top of these, standards such as Bluetooth, Near Field Communications (NFC), and Open Application Program Interface Protocols (API) have enabled a further explosion of connected services that run across these networks. Proprietary technologies can exploit these standards and create their own technology ecosystems of technology products and services. Others can develop open platforms of shared software code and standards that are community based. Secondly, through embedded software technologies, smart fridges, smart printers, smart lighting, smart heating, smart rooms, and connected automobiles – as well as many other devices – have been "enabled" to connect through networks and algorithms to create new kinds of smart services and products. The key step is taken when these smart objects can "talk" to one another and become a sum of integrated experiences that enable new digital workspaces of value. A third aspect of this ecosystem is the aim for interoperable standards. At a basic level, IP addresses, XML, URLs, and other core schemas had to be established in the early internet to enable it to connect in a consistent way with end points in networks, the browsers, and devices. Without a common understanding of standards, no notion of exchange would have been possible. Today, these foundations have moved on to a new level of connection and sharing of digital content for products, services, and social exchanges, thereby creating value ahead of the earlier standards. Furthermore, mobile networks, Wi-Fi, and NFC, to name a few new network standards, are seeking to further add common standards to enable objects in what is termed the Internet of Things to build a new generation of services.

Technology Ecosystem Viewpoint 5: Technology in the Workplace

The digital revolution we have seen in information, operating models, and advanced technologies has the potential to reshape the spaces in which we live and work. A fifth important technological ecosystem view is that of the digital workplace.

There have been four changes affecting the ways physical workplaces have the potential to gain immersive new experiential systems:

- **Sensors and actuators** that measure and affect outcomes in the physical environment.
- **Interactions and visualizations** of information about the environment.
- **Social spaces** that represent the personal private and public personas.
- **Contextual spaces** that define the moment of an event and action in the present, past and future.

Firstly, a range of sensors including those for heat, light, movement, sound, and many stimuli can be placed in rooms, buildings, cars, and city locations. These devices can passively or actively collect and process signals that can be transmitted remotely to a platform in a mobile device, a room or building management system, or a moving vehicle. Secondly, the form in which humans can interact with and visualize this information is now multifarious. A nice phrase to capture this concept is "10s, Tabs, Pads, Boards, Spaces and Places," which refers to the size of the device you can interact with. These can range from hand-held and wearable mobile devices of 10 centimeters or less to tablets and wall-mounted screens, and even to large crowd boards and spaces for "live" advertising and event communications. Large stadium and concert events can have very large-scale place screens for mass visual communications. These capabilities combine to enable different types of online and offline social space gathering, from social meetings to formal working groups and marketplaces. Together they create the potential for tactile, verbal, and augmented feedback that can enhance workplaces.

Technology Ecosystem Viewpoint 6: Enterprise Vendor Technologies

Another key viewpoint of technological ecosystems is the commercial branding and service aspects of digital business. These create real boundaries for commercial and technological products and services depending on how they are bundled and offered to markets and customers.

The definition of "brand" is key in defining how providers of digital technologies denote and define their image in the market. Whether these help or detract, they are a fact of life in the commercial world where image and perceptions of value are key to competitive engagement. There are in fact thousands of commercial, governmental, community, and charitable status companies that emerge, grow, and change over time. The questions is how do they match their products and services to and define them for a given market and set of needs?

Digital technology can be defined by the description of the technologies that matter to the digital enterprise and the IT vendor as well. The marketplace is made up of a plethora of vendors who may be enabled by their vendor capabilities to support their ecosystem of standards, products, and services.

Technology Ecosystem Viewpoint 7: Privacy, Confidentiality, Security, and Trust

Our final viewpoint of technological ecosystems is cyber security and the impact of digital content and its regulation.

Our personal data and what it means to have privacy is fundamentally altered by digitized information about us, the objects we own or interact with, and our relationships to other people, all of which can be copied, transmitted, recoded, reused, and analyzed. The concept of a "digital self" or "digital double" is becoming a reality, as the information that is provided and left online becomes the territory of privacy controls and regulation. Digital information that represents your "digital persona" or "digital self" is a kind of proxy of your physical self. At one extreme we see the marvels of CGI on film that mimic the physical form of the human body and facial features. Yet this kind of virtual reality is different from one's image and personal data being used. The "digital life" is a journey: as we walk down a city street, we may interact with many security cameras, Wi-Fi, and mobile network cells with our smartphones; we may access ATMs or speak or work online, whether on websites or in marketplaces.

The ecosystem of privacy

Many digital technologies have created this privacy ecosystem, and there are numerous questions over how this ecosystem is defined, governed, and regulated. In considering the impact of privacy we can examine the interaction of privacy with confidentiality, security, and trust in an ecosystem context (see Figure 1.4).

In **privacy**, what level and control of data isolation should there be? What level of control should an individual or organization have over access to and use of their data by a third party? What level and control of archive data, access in subpoenas, and data destruction should there be? Should there be the right to be forgotten?

In **confidentiality,** what level and control of data disclosure to unauthorized individuals, entities, or processes should there be? What level and control of intellectual property containment and rights management?

In **trust**, what level and control of authorization and restriction should be provided to an individual or third party to use personal data? What level and control of authenticity to ensure that an entity is what it claims to

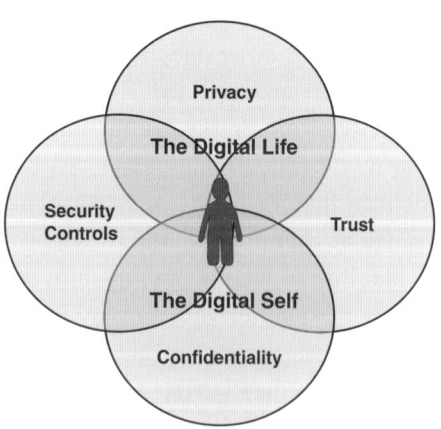

FIGURE 1.4   PCST model of digital privacy

be? What level of perimeterization should there be to define boundaries for personal and corporate trust?

In **security controls**, what level of integrity and persistence of data should there be – with what properties of accuracy and completeness? What level and control of non-repudiation; the ability to prove a claimed event or action and its originating entities? What level of conformity should there be to ensure that privacy requirements are carried out? What level of monitoring and response should there be to planned or unplanned security incidents, for example DDOS (distributed denial of service) or data breach? Should there be a process to determine a system's integrity?

Regulation and cyber threats

The rise in digitally enabled threats and the speed of regulation to counter cyber misuse are key issues of our time and underpin any digital practice, individual responsibilities, and the wider market impact. How legislation will evolve as the "connected self" traverses many formal and informal social, business, and governmental domains remains a hot topic in today's media, and has significant implications for practitioners. Figure 1.4 illustrates a wide range of levels of legislation and domains that the internet and digital services may cut across. The "digital self" may touch many of these domains while the physical self may only be living in one geographical area. The figure shows the impact of digitization on legal and commercial governance, and the implications for the physical and digital self.

There is a big difference between your physical self and physical environment, and what you are aware of in the context of digital technology. The wider digital ecosystem changes a person's privacy, confidentiality, security, and trust domains. What may be termed the "digital self" will in the future need to consider the consequences of digital information and online behaviors that exist as another technologically defined ecosystem. This is already apparent today, as there are many signs of intended and unintended impacts on individuals, social groups, enterprises, governments, and society.

The Practitioners' Digital Enterprise Technology Constituency

We have seen in the previous section the emergence of many types of technologically enabled ecosystems, but it is simplistic to assume that digital is the whole story; it is actually part of wider thoughts about ecosystems. Technological ecosystems span whole markets as well as continents, countries, and industries. Digital technologies can *cluster*, linking across one or many markets and enterprises, or focus on specific social groups and individuals. It is useful to recognize these clusters when we explore the building blocks of a digital enterprise.

> *Super cluster*
>
> A grouping of technologies that span a market or set of markets and economies that can reach and access the physical and enable the digital economy
>
> *Local cluster*
>
> A grouping of technologies that span an enterprise or collection of enterprises and its economic activities

It can been seen that digital technologies exist in one or more of these technology ecosystems. These digital technologies enable a business to cut across supply chains, workplaces, and other technologies to build new value networks and digital capabilities.

In the case studies later in the book we will see several digital technologies that individually or together create different architectural arrangements.

In the "super cluster" technological capabilities are constantly developing and emerging across the local, regional, and global economies.

In our "local cluster" there are those technologies that as practitioners we are concerned about in order to enable and build our digital enterprises. There are many potential types of digital technologies and components that can fit together with the social, business ethical, commercial, and other concerns. From our many case studies there are currently probably *seven leading candidate technologies*. These will of course converge, change, and evolve over time, but our journey begins here in building the digital enterprise. Examples of proprietary definitions of digital technologies include:

- Mobile devices
- Social media
- Cloud computing
- Big data
- Internet of Things
- Machine learning
- Cyber security
- Augmented reality
- Virtual reality
- Artificial intelligence

Chapter Summary

In this chapter we have explored the meaning of technological ecosystems and the development of the digital technology constituency. In the next chapter we will start to unpack the meaning of digitization and begin to define digital workspaces.

Digital Workspace Concepts

Chapter Introduction

In our everyday lives we seek out meaning in the communication and interactions we have, with little thought as to how this works. Yet to a computer the act of natural language processing and "speaking" is a highly complex and difficult task. The subtle nuances of a facial expression, the tone of a human voice, the use of body language in the gesture of a hand or a touch is used to convey much direct and unspoken cultural information. Will machines ever have the empathy to understand and emotionalize these same features? Will machines have the cognitive ability to understand more than direct procedural instructions or to comprehend the ambiguity and intonation that often goes alongside natural language? These are perhaps goals of many cybernetic research projects today; it is a realistic frontier for the development of a union between the physical world and the technological world. This journey is a series of steps in the encoding of basic data into more sophisticated forms of transactions and then on to complex language and representations of the physical world in virtual environments. This journey has already begun, with the explosion in digital data from devices, sensors across the internet, and the myriad of software applications. Through images, emails, video, and web pages, we are describing our lives and the places we visit, live in, and work in.

It is this key idea that sits behind the notion that the physical workplaces we inhabit are being digitized into virtual environments. How do we represent this development as the many devices and sensors collect data, and move this to the internet and the myriad of software applications?

In this chapter we will explore the progress of key ideas in information to describe physical work and what it means for building a digital enterprise. We will examine some theories of information, then introduce ideas about how digitization changes the perception of the physical space and moments in time. We describe these as *spatial* and *temporal* changes that are caused by the characteristics of digital information that we examined in the previous chapter. These features have the ability to change how humans and machines interact with each other and to transform their environments.

This chapter covers the following topics:

- The human–machine interface
- The semiotics ladder
- Contextualization of objects, places, and actions
- The changing space and time of our environment
- Digital capabilities and digital spaces
- Perception and space
- Aesthetics and spaces

The Human–Machine Interface

Semantics is the field of study relating to the meaning of things. The word is derived from the Ancient Greek word σημαντικός (semantikos), "related to meaning, significant," from σημαίνω semaino, "to signify, to indicate," which in turn is from σῆμα sema, "sign, mark, token." The plural is used in analogy with words similar to physics, which was the neuter plural in Ancient Greek and meant "things relating to nature." Semantics is often related to language semantics, where the meaning of human expression through language defines how information is interpreted and communicated. Language is critical to both humans and machines such as computers, both of which need to understand and communicate through a common language notation. Clearly there are many differences between machine code language and human language, and information and meaning are conveyed, interpreted, translated, and enacted in many different ways. To some extent this is one of the core issues facing digitization and human–machine boundaries that this book touches on. Indeed many machine systems involving computation and devices are based on machine-to-machine interaction that does not involve human intermediaries. This does not negate the importance of systems and their human benefits. I am speaking of the differences in semantic notation and communication that are a means to an end, enabling such interfaces and integration to work. At a basic level Figure 2.1 illustrates these interfaces.[1] Human-to-human communication protocols include natural language, written language, signage and visual notations, body language, olfactory language, and augmented language, such as clothing and rituals. These have evolved over many thousands of years and represent the complex nuances of human behavior and societal norms and values. The introduction of mechanization and, importantly, machinery, which enabled

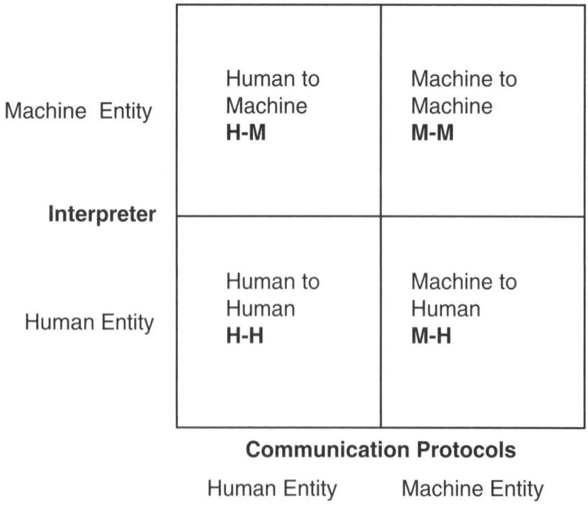

	Human Entity	Machine Entity
Machine Entity	Human to Machine **H-M**	Machine to Machine **M-M**
Interpreter		
Human Entity	Human to Human **H-H**	Machine to Human **M-H**

Communication Protocols

Human Entity   Machine Entity

FIGURE 2.1   **Human–machine boundaries**

human and information communications and the communication and interpretation of the meanings and actions of human and non-human contextual information has made a profound difference.

To some extent this basic determination of machine and human interfaces is misleading in a digital ecosystem, in that there can be many-to-many relationships in the digital world. Many participating websites, content owners, mobile devices, connected systems, and humans represent a more diverse and distributed environment that is more representative of the real world. Millions of interactions are enabled through networks and digital technologies in every minute of the day. It is these collective interfaces that enable a far grander scale of machine-to-machine and human-to-human interaction. Understanding how these ecosystems of digital collectiveness work is a key issue in architecting both digital enterprises and in understanding how economy functions and grows in a digital way. These connections enable a kind of community intelligence that reflects the collective behavior of individuals who are connected in human-to-human communications through a machine interface medium such as a social network.

Both human-to-machine and machine-to-human interfaces have moved rapidly beyond the handset of a telephone or a television in the corner of a room. New visualization systems enabled by digital effects of light, image, sound, and transport can change how machines interact with humans. Smartphones, and embedded sensors in doors, rooms, and cars enable humans to interface with machines increasingly through body movement and status, room location or environment, and with tactile and natural language options as well as touchscreen and text interfaces to exchange and gain information.

The Semiotics Ladder

The modern foundations of meaning and language are typically based on what is termed a semiotic framework, which defines the various components of language, including syntax, semantics, and pragmatics. Semiotics is broadly defined as the study of meaning-making, and while this is primarily to do with the use of signs and symbols, it is often applied to understanding the fundamental building blocks of language and its use in understanding meaning.

The semiotics framework, sometimes called the semiotics ladder, is based on the original work of Professor Charles Morris, an American philosopher,[2] who in 1938 introduced a semiotic model, and Professor Ronald Stamper, who in 1973 expanded it so it applies to information systems (IS) and information technology (IT).[3] Figure 2.2 provides a useful visualization of levels of language meaning from an information systems perspective. Our definition of digital ecosystems is not restricted to information systems or to social aspects in the traditional sense of enterprise software usage, but can encompass a wider set of data and information about things, places, and relationships.

Figure 2.2 is useful in illustrating the bridging of the information system concepts of semantics and the social and physical material worlds that digitization seeks to define.

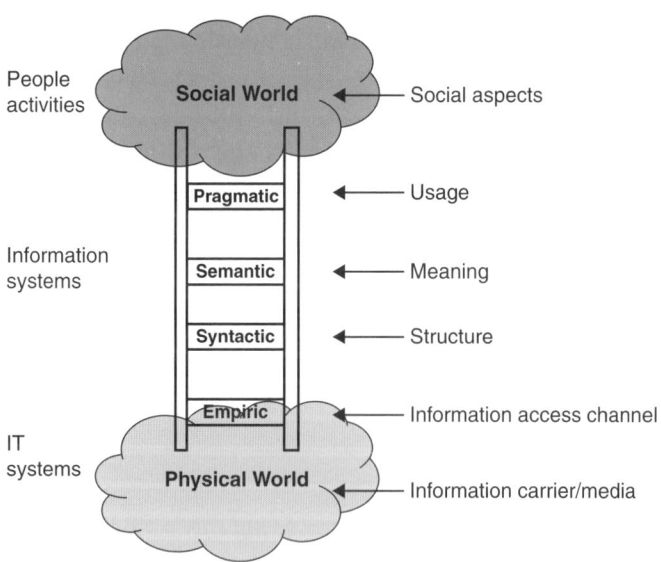

FIGURE 2.2   Semiotics ladder (adapted from Stamper 1973)

Stamper described an elevation of stages in his semiotics ladder, defining the meaning and importantly the outcome context or pragmatics. Fundamentally, at a basic level there would be raw data and information about objects and events, but at higher levels forms of information insight and knowledge about relationships, meaning, and intelligence can be generated and interpreted.

Objects

At its basic level there are objects that exist in this world. The term "morphological" relates to the shape, dimensions, and location of an object. The empirical data of the object are the characteristics that define its dimensionality and properties.

Syntax

The syntactic level is the set of rules that are used to construct a sentence to describe an object. For example in information technology, a data schema is used to describe information about an object. The famous American linguist Noam Chomsky described syntax as the study of the principles and processes by which sentences are constructed in particular languages.[4]

Semantics

The semantics level is the definition of the meaning of information. Semantics is often split into two areas: logical semantics is concerned with making sense, and referring to assumptions about a object or situation; lexical semantics is concerned with the analysis of meaning and the relations between catalogs of words that make up language used to describe mean, the lexicon. In a general sense the field of semantics seeks to provide consistent identifiers of objects and communications, such that the meaning is consistent to all involved in the communication. Endeavors such as the Semantic Web or Web 3.0,[5] and universal tags and indexes seek to establish common standards for objects not just in the structure of the syntax but also aiming to provide standards for the meaning of those objects so that machines can *understand* the objects. Many industries today have universal barcode and credit card payment standards that enable transactions to be executed between parties who only need to understand the protocols and syntax of these standards. Indeed, Tim Berners-Lee described the Semantic Web as a component of a wider movement called the Web 3.0 movement,[6] which aims to establish not just access to the vast data online but make intelligent services available across the net. The goal is the same for digital enterprise and digital ecosystems. While the terms Semantic Web and Web 3.0 are used interchangeably,[7] our definition of digital ecosystems is an implementation of these, but aiming to push into a wider practitioner perspective that takes into account how such concepts fit the real world via the next level, which is pragmatics.

Pragmatics

Pragmatics is about how a situation contributes to the meaning. Pragmatics has sometimes been described as a *meta-language*, which is used to describe specific signs and their usages. In 2007 a semiotics researcher, Daniel Chandler, described the transition of data into information as something done by human beings and not computers. Chandler's contribution was to describe the difference between semantics and pragmatics as the model of representation. Philosophically, it is open to debate whether machines can truly understand meaning, a subject involving artificial intelligence and the meaning of cognitive sentience which is outside our scope here. The key difference between semantics and pragmatics is in the *modality* and representation.[8] *Modality* here refers to the method and the medium through which something is defined in the specific context of a situation. Knowledge alone is not enough to define the meaning of an object. For example, finding and reading a book, visualizing the printed words, then translating this in the brain into what these words mean is the context of "how I am reading." The words themselves are rendered in the book, but are meaningless without the context of the act of reading and then their *interpretation* by the reader. The *meta-language* of how we describe the *pragmatics* of this context is the complete environment: the book, the person, the chair, the room, and the act of reading and understanding. All these things come together in this moment in time, the place and the location in the physical sense.

Earlier we looked at the evolution of information theory and the impact of digitization on this journey. The semiotics ladder is a concept that describes the increasing stages of information and their relationships to meaning, culminating in the reality of knowledge and action in a purposeful way at the pragmatic level. Figure 2.3 illustrates this development of knowledge: it is adapted from work by Ambrose, Ramaprasad, and Rai on the use of distributed knowledge.[9]

The "theory of knowledge" is the span of data and information that describes objects and their relationships up the semiotics ladder. Knowledge becomes more detailed and sophisticated as it represents increasing degrees of connectedness and reality. Likewise, the "theory of being" is developed from defining facts and figures about objects and "things" to increasing levels of representation, showing how these objects and "things" connect with relationships and into meaningful relations and actions. The ability to generate value and worth becomes potentially greater as the levels of information and purposeful action are enabled through these stages of information. This can be seen as a shift in thinking about data and information. Non-contextual data can be regarded as generic data that is not associated with the moment in time or the person or desired action. To move away from being generic to specific about a situation and a person's need is described as being contextual. This is where data is interpreted and converted into meaningful information that is useful and enables purpose to the person or action at that space and time moment. A simple example is when we receive a cold call from a salesperson or we get a list of products from a shop that we may need or want. These are non-contextual, generic to the moment. On the other hand, if we receive an inquiry about a specific product that meets a person's need or want at that moment, it is *contextual*: it is relevant to that situation.

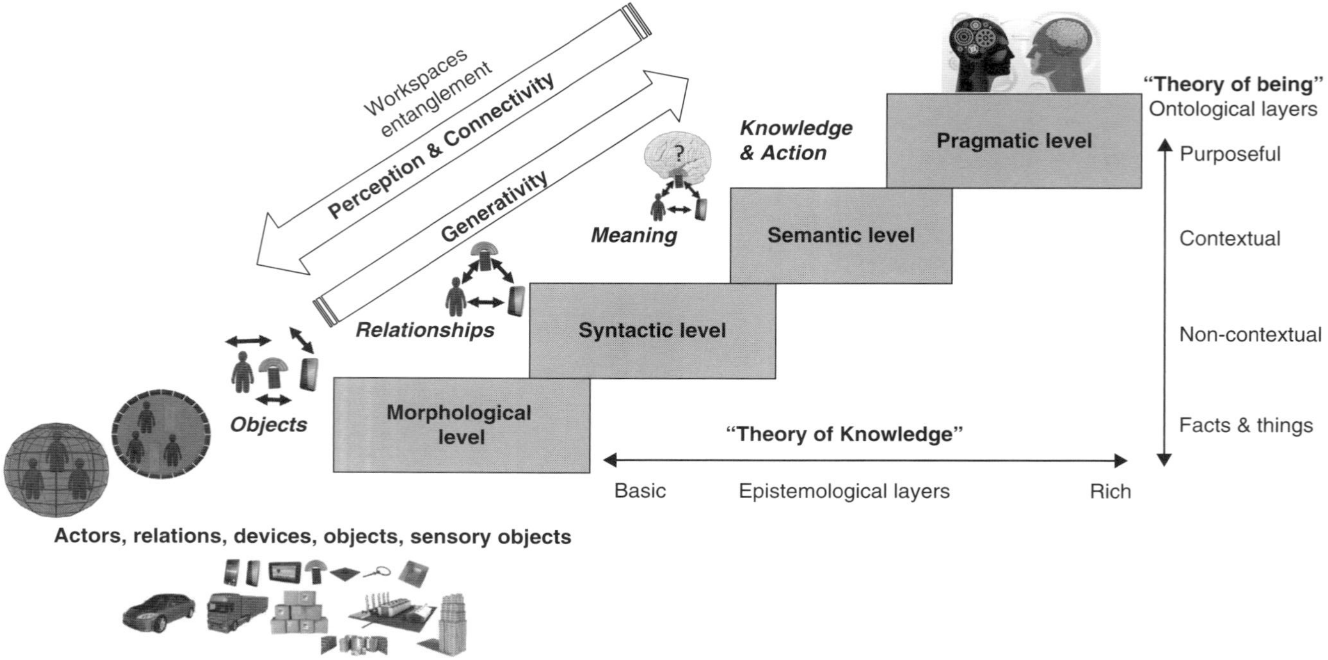

FIGURE 2.3 Evolution of information theory (adapted from P. Ambrose et al. 2003)

"Theory of being"
Ontological layers

Purposeful

Contextual

Non-contextual

Facts & things

Pragmatic level

Semantic level

Knowledge & Action

"Theory of Knowledge"

Syntactic level

Epistemological layers

Meaning

?

Rich

Basic

Morphological level

Relationships

Workspaces entanglement

Perception & Connectivity

Generativity

Objects

Actors, relations, devices, objects, sensory objects

Moving from non-contextual to contextual meaning

- **Facts and things** - the basic raw data and entities.
- **Non-contextual** – generic information about the needs and wants but not directly relatable.
- **Contextual** – specific information to the needs and wants of the moment.
- **Purposeful** – specific information that is actionable for value and worth generating.

Contextualization of Objects, Places, and Actions

As one might expect with semiotics, there may be many different ways to define the meaning of objects: social meaning, implied or emotive meaning, cultural meaning, and others. These differences can be created through different cultural and social norms. Describing an object, or the significance of a statement or gesture, may have different meaning in different cultures and societies. In human communication, the meaning may be direct or implied by nuances. These things are complicated for machines, yet in order for technology to provide context to our living spaces and experiences, it has to climb the semiotics ladder. This can involve basic conversations that name objects and images, and then the language of sentences and commands and a more complex recognition of meaning.

The basic level of semiotics is concerned with defining what an object is. For example, I may describe an object as a "hot cup of coffee" or as "a beverage within a container," but the meaning of my description may not be interpreted the same by all entities. The semiotics ladder helps us illustrate this interpretation as we look at the syntax, semantics, and pragmatics of meaning. In Table 2.1 the context of meaning becomes more sophisticated as we ascend the semiotics ladder.

Ambiguity can exist in the number of permutations of the meaning of "a hot cup of coffee," driven by the nature of what and where the coffee is consumed. The context drives the meaning and purpose.

TABLE 2.1   What is the context of "a hot cup of coffee"?

OBJECT	CONTEXT OF MEANING

	• Syntax – "objects and things"
	  o Size, shape, or the cup
	  o Type of coffee: espresso, Americano, decaf?
	• Semantics – "what"
	  o I am asking for a cup of coffee in a shop
	  o Which coffee am I selecting from a vending machine?
	• Pragmatics – "how"
	  o The cup is hot and you could burn yourself
	  o Do I want a hot coffee or a cold beverage?
	  o The taste of the coffee is hot, like chili
	  o I want to celebrate with a hot cup of coffee

In Table 2.1 we see a cup of coffee, but a machine interface needs to understand and interpret this. Indeed, there have been great strides in image recognition, so much so that airports and search engines can scan images of human faces and complex objects to match patterns for recognition. Further information about objects can be gained by sensors. For example, embedded temperature sensors could enhance information about the object. A "smart cup," for example, could have a built-in heat sensor and another sensor that could detect the liquid's level in the cup. The temperature sensor could automatically detect the temperature and alert the user to its contents, saying "too hot" or "getting cold." The liquid level sensor could order a refill or suggest a different beverage via a connection to a mobile app. Yet for all these advances in sensors, does this enable the semantics and pragmatics of the situation to be fully understood? Are all scenarios for a cup of coffee defined? Are all desired outcomes covered? As we can see, there are many potential outcomes, and it is for this reason that in the design and development of digital workspaces we are seeking to establish better outcomes from information at every level from the objects, content, status, relations to users, and environment. This is a recurring theme that is seen in many modern digital enterprise scenarios, where the issue of digital enablement has moved beyond syntax and basic semantic indexing to more advanced semantics and pragmatics in order to create what we describe as the contextualization of information; that is, information relevant and in context for the user's situation and desired outcomes.

Contextualization

The process by which semantic meaning can be identified and imparted into the situation at hand

At an object level, information standards are continually evolving to define data and transactions such as credit cards, bank accounts, product barcodes, map reference locations, and city and street names. In the digital world, electronic schema standards are also emerging to record and standardize how geographic and merchant data can be recorded and exchanged. Internet traffic and digital messages and images are only possible through the creation and acceptance of common standards. These may be specific to a technology hardware or software or be an "open standard" that is non-proprietary and available for general use.

The key point here is that the use of common syntax is an essential step in being able to create and establish universal agreement. The utopian world view of being able to describe any object in any human or machine language and situation, and it being instantly translated into a universal language, like the "babel fish" in *The Hitchhiker's Guide to the Galaxy* by Douglas Adams,[10] is still yet to fully emerge. Perhaps this may not be so far fetched, as recent announcements by Microsoft and Google have referred to online translation with Skype™ and Google translate, which they say are moving toward real-time multilingual speech conversion.

Every day humans create contextual information to bring meaning to situations and actions. We bring together information from different offline and online sources. We develop social networks both in the physical sense and through online co-presence with others. Community intelligence builds as the exchange of information starts to be contextualized by the grouping of people, either through "tagging" or "by association." Information reinforcement occurs as crowd behavior and viewing habits drive the popularity of certain types of information and events over others.

The Digital User Experience (UX) and Customer Experience (CX)

The connection between human and non-human technologies has been described in recent years as a kind of *digital entanglement*. In the previous section we explored context and meaning. This is important in that it impacts the user experience that is created and interpreted.

Using a holistic approach to UX design and the CX we can start to explore how the human–machine boundary is changing through the process of digitization. What we see is an entanglement of human activities and digital capabilities in organizational routines that are becoming ever more empowering and transformational.[11]

Let us start by exploring the contexts of digital entanglement. I will use the following definitions:

User Experience (UX)

The interaction of the human and a device or sensor through a user interface (UI) to affect the human-experienced outcomes. This is defined as the UX agency of the device or sensor in the context of the location and time. This agency can also apply to other forms of actor, including non-living objects such as software program agents that work with the device or sensor autonomously by a machine protocol or algorithm, or semi-autonomously through control of a human.

Customer Experience (CX)

The human in the context of their living environment and the human-experienced outcomes caused by interaction with other humans and objects in that environment context, location, and time.

TABLE 2.2   Space, time, context example definitions

Multiple CX and UX Contexts		
Space – where	**Time – when**	**Semantic – what**
• The location of the coffee cup • The location of the coffee table • The location of the coffee shop • The location of the road where the coffee shop is sited • The location of the town or city where the road and coffee shop are sited • The region • The country	• The moments before deciding to get a coffee • The moment of selecting the location of the coffee • The moment of selecting the type of coffee • The moment of paying for the coffee • The moment when the coffee is taken to and placed on the table • The moment the coffee is consumed • The moments after the coffee is consumed	• Motivations before the need to obtain a coffee • The searching for the type of coffee required • The cost and time of travel to the coffee shop • The social meeting of others who might be in the same coffee shop • The payment methods for the coffee • The types of facilities in the coffee shop • The other services in the coffee shop following coffee consumption • The related services outside the coffee shop

Using our cup of coffee example we might describe user experience context in three ways (see Table 2.2).

1. The spatial location of where we might order and drink a cup of coffee.
2. The time before, during, and after we consume the coffee.
3. The semantically described reasons why and how we consume the cup of coffee.

We will see as we explore the digitization of space, time, and semantic meaning to create multiple contexts, that things can become radically different as the virtual world entangles with physical objects and places.

A day in the life of living next door to a "smart photocopier"

In the room next door to my office there is a "smart photocopier" that is connected to the internet. The machine automatically detects when its ink cartridge is getting low and sends out an email to reorder a new printer cartridge. Ordering online stocks is fast and convenient, and as a consumable item does not need

> *to be authorized for purchase approval or regularly checked by operators, the embedded sensors in the photocopier are able to do this job. The following day the cartridge parcel arrives by recorded delivery, but no one is available to collect and sign for it. I offer to sign for it in the absence of anyone else available, and it is placed in my room with a note left under the door saying "I signed for the photocopy in the absence of any available human..."*

This story shows us that there is a big difference between UX and the overall CX. Whereas the UX is the checking, ordering, and delivery of the photocopier supplies, the end-to-end flow of different actors, organizational departments, and work routines affect the overall outcome of the CX. It may be a trivial example, but it illustrates that UX and CX design is a key part of enabling the smart photocopier, smart fridge, or smart TV to automate steps in the reordering of components or to make suitable suggestions.

As we will see in the digital enterprise case studies, though, it is possible to create digital workspaces that can directly affect outcomes for individuals and an enterprise.

For example, multi-modal traffic and transport arrival times can be optimized; patient healthcare delivery can be remotely supported; retail products and metropolitan services can be enabled with smart technology to assist the smooth operation of living spaces and consumption. These are increasingly linked by digital technologies that affect economic and social outcomes. Digital entanglement matters in the way that context is enabled in objects, locations, and an organization's routines and procedures.

Let us start to explore this digital entanglement as a way to define workspaces that are enabled through digital technologies. We can divide this into social, business, and knowledge contexts to illustrate how this is changing physical workplaces into digital workspaces.

Social context

Building on the cup of coffee analogy, let us return to a contextual setting. In the social context there can be many devices and sensors that are immersed in and connected to the social experience.

Examples of digital workspaces can include smart rooms and building facilities that enable social gatherings with ambient lighting, humidity controls, and wireless connectivity.

Room artifacts such as smart tabletops with interactive displays, wireless charging, and location tracking for meeting coordination and time productivity tracking.

Room walls and windows can become dynamic viewing boards for virtual telepresence meetings and information display communication boards.

Wearable technology can monitor social connections and shared social experiences.

Multiple contexts can drive customer outcomes to gain better social experience and higher productivity of meetings and social interactions.

Business context

The presence of consumers and providers in the immediate physical location as well as digital connectivity to supply chains of products and services enable new commercial, technical, and ethical models.

Digital workspaces can develop automated reordering and stock control of products and services.

Dynamic services can be created for customers in the context of a meeting place through personalized recommendations and dynamic "menus" and promotions, to assist and augment the customer experience.

Smart point of sale devices and sensors can be used in fixed locations and in smartphone applications to drive service efficiencies and customer loyalty programs.

Location facilities can create immersive brand images, smart art, and dynamic advertising boards.

Information about visitors and consumption habits can be collected and analyzed for improvements of productivity and targeted services.

Employee smart badges and wearable assistant devices can help provide employee assistance and tracking.

Multiple contexts across business locations, outlets, and points of customer contact can drive improved customer experience outcomes. Business operations and partner collaboration can be augmented to create co-benefits and co-innovation across product and service locations.

Knowledge context

Today mobile devices and embedded sensors allow a potential revolution in the ability to collect and bring knowledge and insight to locations and contexts remotely. The knowledge context of digital entanglement has never been felt more keenly in the way social and business behavior models have shifted thanks to the use of digital technology.

Examples of knowledge augmentation in context are wide and varied, including mobile and tablet devices with local proximity connectivity in order to sense their environment.

Rooms, buildings, and whole cities can have connected spaces covered by mobile and wireless infrastructure with telemetry for heat, light, CO_2, nitrogen, and consumption and wastage data.

Wearable technology can create wellbeing and health information and behavior incentives as well as monitoring and driving social value.

Objects including automobiles, engines, buses, trains, ships, and aircraft extend the envelope of digitization to include services on the move through local, regional, and global travel.

Proximity between local and remote locations can span and connect social information-sharing.

The many contexts of knowledge create new forms of customer experience outcomes.

Building digital capabilities from digital spaces

In this section we have explored the ideas of information theory and concepts of contextualization. Digital technologies pervade physical locations and objects, creating new user and customer experiences.

One goal is understanding how this digital entanglement works in practical terms.[12]

- How do the organizational routines become digitized?
- How is this scalable across multiple contexts?
- How do human activities and digital capabilities become entangled across contexts?
- How does technology become entangled in patterns of practice we can learn and share?

The next step is to start to define how the enterprise builds these digital workspaces.

Cognitive understanding and co-presence are no longer just in physical moments of human-to-human presence, but can be created and "held in virtual space" through digital entanglement.

Interpretation is not a one-way process. The act of participating in the activity by definition makes you part of that activity.

In developing a working digital architecture for a digital enterprise we need to break the situation down into its constituent building blocks. It has been long considered that "Understanding the building block is requisite to designing the wall."[13]

Semantic construction is a key concept in complex systems analysis and requirements management.[14,15] This book seeks to define principles from practitioners to show how digital systems are constructed.

In the next section we will explore the evolution of enterprise architecture and show how digital technologies are changing the nature of enterprise technology design.

We will then explore how the concepts of contextualization are put to practical use in the design of workspaces, the digital content, and its use through time. These new digital workspaces are a building block for a modern digital enterprise and the digital economy.

Enterprise Software Practice Evolution

For a practitioner in business systems development, the use of technology to enable new types of business processes is at the core of architectural systems engineering.

Selection, functional design, coding development, testing, and migration to the production environment are all key. With digital technologies involved in website design and mobile applications, for example, the use of rapid prototyping techniques, often described as *fourth generation software techniques*, use stored software code and visualization of the end user screen has rapidly changed systems development. These tools and practices have enabled the development time for general commercial software in some cases to become a matter of days and weeks.

This is not to say that all software development is rapid: large and complex enterprise applications can have many software modules and components. Examples of these in outliers of the gaming industry use advanced graphics design, and the advances in complex data analytics require specialist skills and resource-intensive computational processing power and data management. What is changing through digitization is the enabling of rapid enterprise-class software development.

Back in 2009, Salesforce.com was reported at a press analyst event by CEO, Marc Benioff, to have more than 55,000 enterprise customers, 1.5 million individual subscribers, running on 30 million lines of third-party code, and hundreds of terabytes of data all running on 1,000 machines. Amazon's

Web Services, in comparison, runs on 100,000 machines.[16] Today these are much larger: for example, in 2013 Google, with the market value of $290 billion, has over 12 data centers around the world processing 20 petabytes of user-generated data per day, running 24 hours a day, seven days a week.[17,18] The technology ecosystem includes 900 million Android devices and has passed 1 million Android apps.[19,20]

Data analytics are now a major business tool for social business behavior analysis, for retailers, social media, financial services, and many other industries. For example, Walmart reportedly handles more than 1 million customer transactions every hour containing more than 2.5 petabytes (2,560 terabytes) of data. Walmart Labs have used this data to create products such as "Social Genome" for improved semantic search in its e-commerce and m-commerce channels, "ShoppyCart" for social gift suggestions, and "Get on the Shelf", a crowdsourcing product ideas model that drives new customer product experiences.[21,22,23]

In financial services, global payments systems provider MasterCard aggregates and analyzes 65 billion transactions from 15 billion cardholders in 201 countries to identify business and consumer trends. In a briefing at the GigaOM Structure Data 2013 Conference in New York, Gary Keams, Group Executive, Information Services, MasterCard Worldwide, explained how big data is used by retailers to help drive co-brand growth and core business sales.[24]

Apart from social influence models, big data analytics is being used in extreme speed and volume scenarios that are made possible by advanced computing technology and its lower cost. Real-time transactions in financial services' high-frequency trading (HFT) compute rapid trading decisions and automated fund timing, price, and quantity of buy and sell orders, in many cases initiating the order automatically by computer algorithm. Such machine-to-machine (M2M) processing has caused some industry observers to raise concerns about the control of trading and its impact on the stock market.

Machine learning (ML) algorithms are not limited to the financial market. We regularly use embedded sensors and embedded machine code algorithms in smartphones and tablets to get feedback from location data, weather forecasts, fitness apps, and heart rate monitors. In the automotive industry, the "connected car" has an array of electronic embedded sensors that may affect between 30 and 50 different on-board and external systems. The president of Ford, Stephen Odell, says, "Cars are the smartphones of the future. There are many untapped opportunities for mobile to play a role in advanced automated driving."[25]

In the field of large data set analysis, there have been high-profile examples in astronomy, earth climate change forecasting, and medical research. NASA's Large Synoptic Telescope Survey starts in 2016 and will collect 140 terabytes every five days.[26] A recent OECD report into the cost of decoding the human genome can be digitized in less than a day, a feat that would have been cost prohibitive ony a few years ago. DNA sequencers have divided the sequencing cost by 10,000 in the last ten years, which is 100 times quicker than the reduction in cost predicted by Moore's Law.[27]

Evolution of Software Techniques – Toward "Digital Convergence"

The speed of computation and digital data growth is predicted to accelerate in the next few years. The increase in high-volume data versus practical considerations such as latency, error rates of data quality and accuracy, computational accuracy, and network bandwidth to cope with the volume of data collection and aggregation, will be critical to the performance of these systems.[28] This increasing scale and complexity will impact how digital technologies can perform effectively. Yet we must also embrace ideas that represent the new world and not be constrained by the old definitions of physical materiality.[29] David Thorburn, MIT Professor of Literature and Director of the MIT Communications Forum, wrote about this in *The Web Paradox* about the contradictory nature of the web (internet).

> *The computer encourages joining, interaction, sharing, the creation of communities of interest; yet it is also congenial to our uncivic preferences for isolation, the avoidance of human*

contact, solipsism, "lurking", voyeurism. Through its power to confer anonymity, it feeds instincts for scandal, revenge, name-calling, surveillance, pornography.

It is the best of Webs, the worst of Webs. It promises, simultaneously, to become the Agora, True Democracy, but also Big Brother. Do I contradict myself? says the American poet, very well then I contradict myself. I am large, I contain multitudes.

It is easy to misconceive the import of such discourse about the Web's contradictory nature, and especially its power to threaten such vital conceptual and psychological boundaries as "near" and "far," "presence" and "absence," "body" and "self," "real" and "artificial."

We must understand the impact of the digital and social impact of *the web when we add the term "virtual" that is now fundamental to our experience of computers: virtual environment, virtual community, virtual reality.*

David Thorburn, MIT, 1998, extract from *The Web Paradox.*[30]

As practitioners using the web of technologies, it is a path we must travel to navigate through the endless possibilities. As practitioners we have to understand how the early stages of software code development and hardware have evolved and will continue to advance into the new virtual environments, virtual communities, and virtual reality that they are enabling. Many of the case studies in this book are testament to the fact that digital technology has progressed from a technological foundation to a truly immersive experience.

In practice there are many software and hardware techniques that are in evidence today that cross between "developer-led" software coding practices and the "consumer-led use" of devices and infrastructure. As a result, software and hardware are converging to leverage the old software coding styles and the new performance of scalable hardware architectures "in the cloud." Gary Lyon, Chief Innovation Officer of MasterCard Labs, MasterCard Worldwide, described this phenomenon as "digital

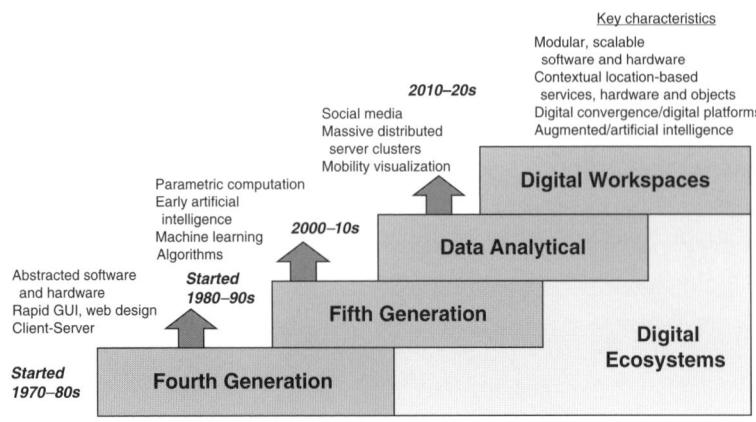

FIGURE 2.4 Software and hardware development techniques

convergence."[31] It is the bringing together of digital solutions and services into the place and context of your customers and partners. These have emerged from the earlier foundations of software and hardware engineering practices into the converged physical and virtual world of user experience and social business analytics, and beyond into digital platforms. This can be seen as a journey of four distinct ideas or phases in information systems technology development, spanning technological to business and then into social and societal convergence (see Figure 2.4).

Fourth-Generation Software Developments and Techniques

Fourth-generation software techniques are based on software development platforms and code tools that broadly aim to rapidly develop software code independent of the hardware platform. Fourth-generation languages can perform a range of program tasks from database queries and report generation to data manipulation and mathematical analysis as well as Graphical User Interface (GUI) design. Languages such as SQL, ABAP, FOCUS, OpenROAD, SAS, and code generators Perl, Python, Ruby, and many others are available today. Business Process Management (BPM) has been a strong advocate of this style of development, using graphical notation to develop workflow algorithms with BPML (Business Process Modeling Language), BPEL (Business Process Execution Language), and various software-specific languages in BPMS (Business Process Management Systems) tools. BPM is sometimes described not as software engineering but a variation focused on business and technologists who are designing how work operations function and the user tasks engineering involved in achieving this, where the software is but one part of this enablement.[32]

Examples of fourth-generation software and hardware developments and techniques:

- Scrum software development methodology, which used an interactive and incremental agile software development framework. The direct user or representative worked together with the software developer to rapidly define requirements and prototype the screens and workflows. The key feature is that it progressively builds solutions.
- UX development methodology, where the focus is on human user interaction. Techniques such as "user journeys" and "wireframes" are used to design how the user uses the system to enable user experience outcome.
- Fourth-generation languages have a high level of abstraction from the hardware they run on, and therefore have high level natural language.
- Cross-platforming, where code written to run on Apple iOS, for example, can also run on Android, Symbian, Blackberry, or Windows phones in the mobile device operating system.
- Software development kit (SDK) uses prebuilt code and visual "drag-and-drop" features to design database queries, report generation, screen interaction, data manipulation, high-level graphics capabilities, and automated generation of the Graphical User Interface (GUI) or web page development using advanced software tools.
- "WYSIWYG," the what you see is what you get principle of design and visual rendering, so that the final result on the end device matches the mobile, tablet, or large-screen device. The code is able to detect and change format dynamics with different device screen sizes.

- Integrated Development Environment (IDE), where the code libraries and distribution are managed automatically.
- Automated Deployment is automatically generated software code, which compiles and produces the code for use in the product.
- Disposable software, where code is generated rapidly, and rather than being edited any changes can be rewritten automatically.

Fifth-Generation Software Developments and Techniques

Fifth-generation software development techniques are based on solving problems using constraints given to a program, rather than using an algorithm written by the programmer. Whereas fourth-generation languages are designed to build specific programs, fifth-generation languages are designed to make the computer solve a given problem without the programmer. Fifth-generation languages are used mainly in artificial intelligence, and examples include Lisp, Prolog, STRIPS, and POP-11. The development of AI concepts has seen the rise of neural network computing and the move toward cognitive computing, a branch of cybernetics. Robotic sensors and actuators in seeing, sensing, scanning, and in self-driving autonomous units and manipulation devices have pushed the boundary of spatial, auditory, and visual awareness in computing.[33]

Examples of fifth-generation software and hardware developments and techniques:

- Parallel Processing, using multi-core computing processors and technics such as multi-threading processing with specialized software operating systems to execute complex computation found in supercomputing and high-performance computing (HPC). Parallel process in this context is used in parallel computing, a technique for conducting complex calculations by splitting them into individual smaller parts and processing them in parallel, then recombining to gain the final result.[34]

- Logic Processing, a mathematical approach used in ProLog to determine whether or not a given statement follows logically from other given statements.
- Heuristic Processing, a technique designed for solving a problem more quickly when classic methods are too slow, or for finding an approximate solution when classic methods fail to find any exact solution. This is achieved by trading optimality, completeness, accuracy, or precision for speed, obtaining faster overall computational results.
- Neural networks or neural network computing is an artificial set of computational "nodes" based on the concept of the neuron structure of the brain. It is designed as a computational model based on the biological brain to solve certain kinds of problems, typically pattern recognition, which are "easy-for-a-human, difficult-for-a-machine" tasks. Applications for this range from optical character recognition (turning printed or handwritten scans into digital text) to facial recognition.[35]
- Cognitive computing is a methodology for computing complex situations that are characterized by ambiguity and uncertainty to provide human-assisted context support. It uses a combination of technologies and techniques to link data analysis and adaptive page displays to adjust the content to the particular type of audience, the context. Cognitive computing systems seek to redefine the role of the computation as an assistant or coach for the user, and they may act virtually autonomously in many problem-solving situations.[36]
- Swarm intelligence is an approach to using self-organized systems by decentralized collective behavior.[37] It is a form where robotic agents with basic rules are able to act as a multi-agent of behavior. This behavior is found in nature in examples that include ant colonies, bird flocking, animal herding, bacterial growth, and fish shoals. Human crowd behavior can exhibit swarm behavior and social preference clustering based on the collective behavior and interactions of a crowd. "Swarm prediction" can be used in the context of forecasting problems.
- Robotics is a field that involves advances in electro-mechanical manipulation and environmental augmentation through artificial automated machine response. Many examples of industrial and commercial robots may be seen, ranging from manufacturing, materials handling, and

basic home appliances. The term "android" or a synthetic organism designed to look and act like a human, especially with a body that has a flesh-like resemblance has remained largely in the realm of science fiction. Recent advances in software-based avatars emulating a virtual person, as described in the Turing test,[38] and cybernetics have aimed to provide early examples of realistic humanoid robots and human empathetic behavior emulation.[39]

Data Analytical Software Developments and Techniques

Data analytical software development techniques have pushed past the restrictions of slower relational databases to process large quantities of data. "Big data," as it is generically termed, provides a wide range of correlations and insight and services beyond the transactional and informational aspects of data. To some extent, this has emerged from the use of fourth-generation languages' mathematical computation requirements and fifth-generation languages' attempts to calculate correlations. These have converged with emerging new hardware in operating systems and massive scalable storage, memory, and computational clusters. These capabilities, a branch of high-performance computing and supercomputing, have brought large-scale commercial data analytics into everyday reach of individuals and enterprise to provide truly remarkable capabilities. The advances in analytical methods have gone beyond taking multi-dimensional views of databases and now include natural language processing, generic algorithms, machine learning, signal processing, simulation, and time series analysis. Examples of big data code bases include R, Python, SQL, Java, and SAS. Types of big data storage and databases include NoSQL, Hadoop, HBase, AWS, and simpleDB. NewSQL examples are MemSQL, ScaleBase, VoltDB, and SAP Hana. Big data file management examples include Hadoop and EMC Greenplum. Big data deals with very large unstructured data sets, and is dependent on rapid analytics, with answers provided in seconds. The largest real-time big data practitioners – Google, Facebook, Apple – run what are known as *hyperscale computing environments.*[40] This term refers to specialized stripped-down hyperscale storage that provides rapid, efficient expansion to handle big data use cases, such as web serving and database applications.[41]

Examples of big data software and hardware developments and techniques:

- Big data file management system describes a specific type of software system for controlling files that are optimized to the massive scale and volume found in big data sets.
- NoSQL is a type of database designed for large scalable structured and unstructured data storage and retrieval. Typically these databases use BASE principles (basically available, soft state, eventually consistent properties) in which the data and transactions are not rigorously managed by the file system. Processing data accepts partial complete transactions at a given time but these are eventually consistent. This is different to ACID transactions (Atomicity, Consistency, Isolation, Durability properties) in traditional relational databases in which essentially every transaction is checked for consistency. A main benefit of NoSQL is that data does not need to fit a particular database schema: for structured and unstructured data there is no fixed data model allowing flexibility for the enterprise to access and use large data sets. Features of NoSQL databases and file management systems enable fast highly scalable "big data" processing.
- NewSQL is a type of modern relational database that is designed to provide similar scalable processing performance as NoSQL for transactional ACID data. A term "in-memory" database is a NewSQL approach where the complete database is held in operating memory to enable rapid access and computational processing speeds.
- Data Fabric is a general term given to defining the data collecting, data aggregation, and processing of large-scale data sets. The fabric denotes the scope and sources of data brokerage and orchestration to obtain and render the data in a useful form for analytical processing.
- Visualization refers to techniques for the presentation and communication of data in a graphical format. Data visualization enables large-scale data analysis to be better understood and represented for human

understanding and usage. Popular examples include social media network graphs, displaying the social relationships of associated clusters in social networks. The term infographics refers to techniques to represent key data with graphical projections and color. Many data visualization techniques use interactive graphics to create dynamic content driven by the user that acts together with a user interface, typically by touchscreen.

- Generic algorithms (GA) is a search heuristic that mimics the process of natural selection where a hypothesis is tested and iterated based on best fit, inheritance, mutation, selection, and crossover combinations of solutions to converge to a best solution. The GA technique is used in many engineering, economics, chemistry, and research areas to calculate design solutions that would be highly complex by conventional analysis and calculations.

- Natural language processing (NLP) seeks to use human linguistics for the interaction between humans and computers. There are several uses today in voice recognition and voice translation by computer services through smartphones and cloud-based translation services. Spoken instructions for search and queries or basic operations for assisted living and mobile device operations are available today. Huge differences still exist between translation and interpretation of stored instructions and actual cognitive understanding by machines.

- Simulation refers to methods for creating 2D and 3D representations of physical data to create "synthetic" representations of objects of physical environments for analysis and prediction. One of the major areas of big data is in its use of contextual forecasting to predict scenarios of possible future outcomes. Examples in social media include crowd behavior for riot control, police assessments, forecasting weather patterns, and tornado alerts: just some of the many areas for simulation analysis.

- Signal processing is the area that relates to data collection from sensors and other devices that generate analog as well as digitized signals. Signals include sound, electromagnetic radiation, images, video, acceleration, gravity (three-axis accelerometer), gyroscopic, rotational vector, vibration (seismology), financial signal, and sensor readings; for example, biological measurements such as electrocardiograms, control system signals, and telecommunication transmission signals.

In the Internet of Things this represents a huge area of data collection and automation from M2M and human-to-machine (H2M, M2H) interfaces. In signal processing, the ability to manage abnormal signals for emergency events or data errors are important. This relates to techniques including "signal sensitivity range" and "signal damping" to manage and filter background or non-essential "noise."

- Machine learning (ML) is the study of machines that can learn from data and adapt its analysis and reaction in current and future processing, rather than following explicit programmatic rules. There are many types of machine learning including "supervised learning," where examples of inputs and desired outputs "teach" the machine learning algorithm to improve its response. "Unsupervised learning" is where similar inputs or clusters or a range of data are used to create pattern reinforcement to drive toward a specific improvement goal. In "reinforcement learning" a computer program interacts with a dynamic environment in which it must perform a certain goal (such as driving a vehicle), without a teacher explicitly telling it whether it has come close to its goal or not. Machine learning is used in many embedded systems in control machines for automotive vehicles, autopilots, aerospace engine diagnostics, and a range of other industrial machines.
- Cloud-hosted big data instances enable rapid start-up of data analytics clusters for on-demand use.
- Real-time data stream processing, such as Amazon Kinese™, is used to process information in real time, from sources such as website clickstreams, marketing and financial information, manufacturing instrumentation and social media, and operational logs and metering data.
- Data warehouses and data marts typically run offline analyses.

Digital Workspaces

The boundaries of technology and the physical world change when considering the placement of digital technologies in our everyday lives. This positioning in space has several new transformational properties that enable the physical space to digitally converge with a virtual space view.

Fields of view – PEC – physical, extended, contextual model

At first glance this can be defined as a technology-based definition of extensions to the physical environment and objects within it. Early digitization started to define and collect basic data about products, services, and rooms, and was filled with potential for content for web and mobile (see Figure 2.5).

This is a practical field of view for the building of digital solutions into workplaces.

- How do devices work in the location?
- Where do we place sensors to monitor or augment the environment?
- How do we use the floors, tables, walls, and ceiling to create new information living surfaces?
- How do the "actors," humans, and objects placed in the environment interact with and utilize the digitization of the environment?

But as we consider the third dimension of contextualization of this workplace, the properties of digitization start to potentially change the physical space and time of the moment. Information from other physical locations can be brought together simultaneously to a physical location through

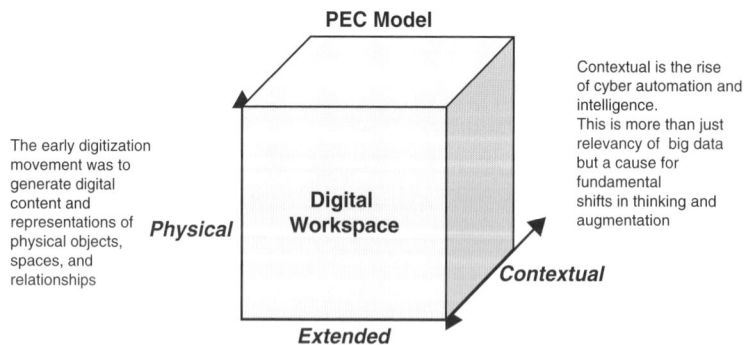

PEC Model

The early digitization movement was to generate digital content and representations of physical objects, spaces, and relationships

Physical

Digital Workspace

Contextual is the rise of cyber automation and intelligence. This is more than just relevancy of big data but a cause for fundamental shifts in thinking and augmentation

Contextual

Extended

The ability to digitally extend to moving objects, transport, and to further more connect and see across geographies is more than the "death of distance." It is a profoundly different movement of spatial and temporal changes that digital technologies can transform physicality into new virtual workspaces

FIGURE 2.5   Fields of view PEC – physical, extended, contextual – model

digital technology, creating a kind of "virtual information". Information in the present can also search information from the past or be projected into the future by seeking alternatives. Using digital technologies it is possible to contextualize this information to the specific moment of the place and its environmental circumstances. This information is from the *digital ecosystem* we introduced earlier that surrounds the networks and devices connected to activities in a location. We explored this in vertical and horizontal value chains, and saw it and the value network ecosystem as examples of how these connected spaces can be built across business process and marketplaces.

Digital ecosystem

A connected convergence of technologies in a market and business activity that enables new consumer, business, and market performance and user experience.

Value network ecosystem

A collection of value activities that may connect to many vertical or horizontal markets, customers, and providers that represent its members of the enterprise ecosystems. The value network represents the enterprise value system, creating and sharing co-benefits through the constituency of members it connects with in its ecosystem.

Digital ecosystems and digital enterprise are in part made up of PEC dimensions. They have digital content about physical objects and spaces but also connectivity to devices, sensors, and software applications that start to enable contextual processing of information to create and enable value in the network of connections.

Digitization Transformation Viewpoint Perspectives

While digitization in PEC enables workspaces, properties of digitization often change the physical location and timeframes, affecting what it is possible to connect.

Digitization changes the physical and virtual locational space dimension and the time, the temporal dimension. Put simply, the physical location you are in while reading this page may be connected to other virtual locations through the internet. You can read this in the present, but you could also access past pages or find information not on this page by searching the internet. In this sense the digital experience is different from the physical one in that space and time are a convergence of physical and virtual environments.

This presents a new kind of mindset that as practitioners we are starting to see with the emerging impact of new digital systems architecture design. A way in which to consider this aspect is to explore the impact of digitization of time, space, and the meaning of content, the semantics of the moment (see Figure 2.6).

We define this as the spatial, temporal, and contextual (STC) dimensions of the digital workspace.

- Spatial
- Temporal
- Contextual (Semantic)

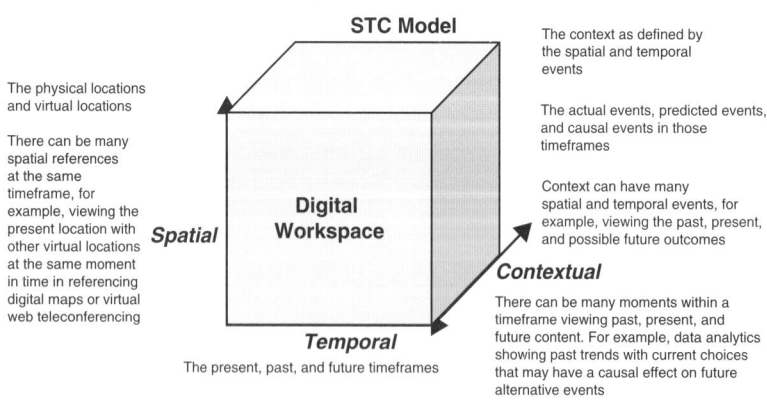

FIGURE 2.6   Field of view of an STC – spatial, temporal, contextual – model

Spatial Field of Information View

Spatial transformation is perhaps the simplest of digitalization concepts brought about by the vast scaling of the internet infrastructure architectures and growth of data and connectivity and devices. The "network effect" is that information across many geographic locations can be digitally transmitted to potentially any physical location. In this sense many physical locations can be virtualized and their information shared simultaneously in any other virtual or physical location (see Figure 2.7).

This changes the potential view or multiple views of information that we can gain about one or many spaces while in one physical place. This is not just through the transmission of digital pictures but involves the information and meaning of the content and location itself. We see this every day with satellite navigation and combined multimedia broadcasts that combine physical and virtual location data into a combined perspective with a special orientation (see Figure 2.8).

From a transformational perspective this changes the *spatial information field of view* from immediate sensory information of the first-person viewpoint into the potential to "see" and interact with collective community information. It also enables third-person perspectives of a wider information field of view containing markets, communities, and global events.

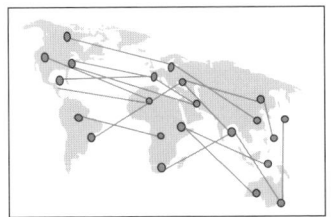

First person viewpoint   Collective person viewpoint   Third person viewpoint

FIGURE 2.7 Spatial views of view

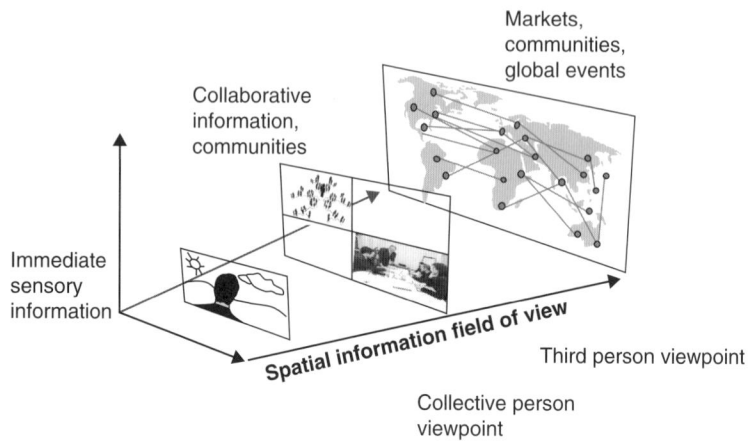

FIGURE 2.8   Spatial information field of view

Semantic Field of Information View

With spatial information it is now possible to view the set of information relating to a specific context, or meaning, from a combination of different sources of information. The digitization of data has followed a path from physical data to a term called "metadata" that *describes information about other information*. With digital technologies that use sensors and data analytics, new forms of metadata about groups of names and activities of communities are collected. Information and their relationships to groups of names and activities or individuals can be generated directly or through analytical inference and future predictions. A buzzword "hyperdata" has emerged that describes a even wider set of information perspectives, combining data and information from many local and global sources to enable large-scale population samples or whole population analysis (see Figure 2.9).

Semantics means that with such data, metadata, and hyperdata perspectives new transformational perspectives are enabled, thanks to the way in which digital technologies can contextualize a moment, something that is physically impossible through human capabilities and local senses (see Figure 2.10).

The semantic information field of view can extend physical information in a contextual situation to include collective intelligence and augmented or artificial intelligence drawing on new forms of semantic data that are generated in the digital ecosystem.

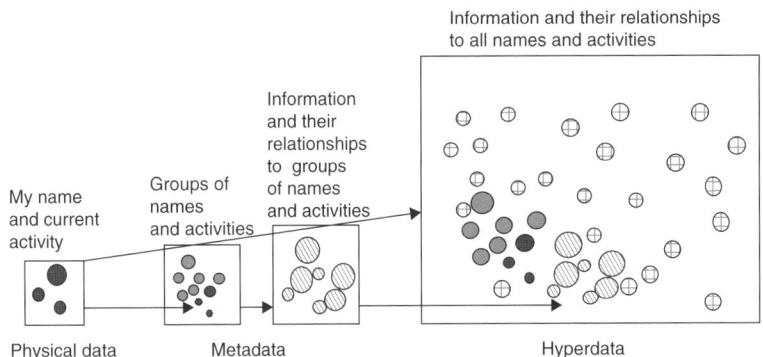

FIGURE 2.9 / **Physical data, metadata, and hyperdata**

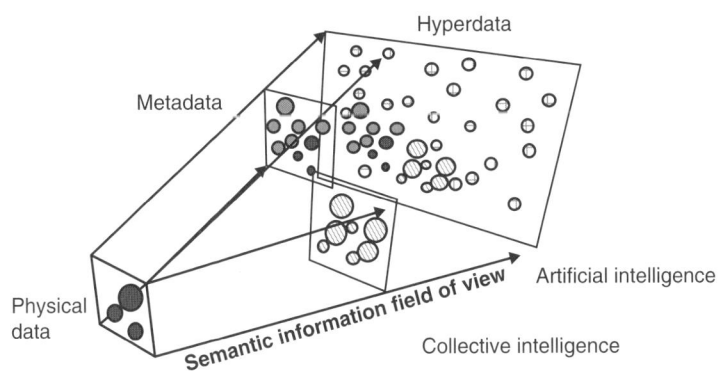

FIGURE 2.10 / **Semantic information field of view**

Temporal Information Field of View

Temporal transformation is probably the hardest concept to grasp.

Human existence occurs in the present, the moment of now. Yet we can remember the past and to some extent our immediate future is before us and known. Events and decisions shape how we move from one time-frame to another (see Figure 2.11).

In the digitization of information some "strange" potential properties emerge, in that we can preserve and record what has happened in the past, and predict and even change the future. This is more than a static picture frame timeline of your post on a social network website. In defining digital content we can create contextual content that continues to co-exist with us in the present. Videos, discussions, and decisions can be preserved and taken with you on mobile devices, websites, and social networks, and "feed back" like a time loop into the present. Furthermore, we can simulate future possible outcomes. We can simultaneously modulate and create alternative outcome choices (see Figure 2.12).

To some extend this is the long tail economic effect first described by Chris Anderson, editor of *Wired* magazine,[42] where many possible choices and outcomes can be made because "everything is available." There are constraints in availability, but this also has a profound potential in the ability to have temporal hindsight and foresight in the present because of

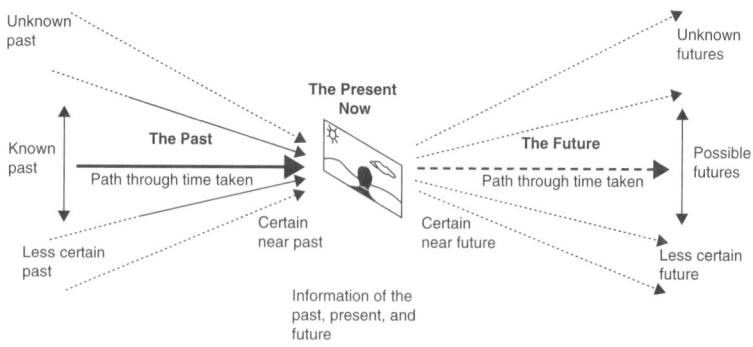

FIGURE 2.11   The present now, pasts, and futures

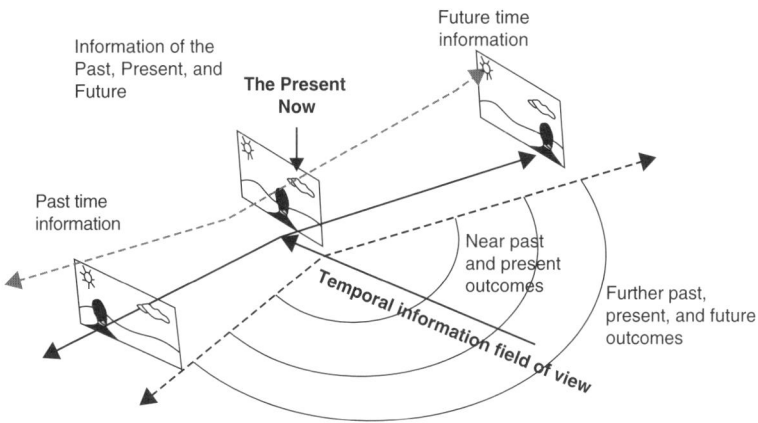

Temporal Ecosystems

FIGURE 2.12 Temporal information field of view

digitization of moments, events, and services. The long tail of availability can also look back at past consumption behavior and look forward to predicted consumption needs and outcomes.

Convergence of Digitization in Physical and Virtual Space and Time

This is not magic, but digitization is significant in its ability to change society and services and the experiential existence for humans. Digital transitions are *transmutational* in that they don't just disrupt innovation in the present moment but alter the very fabric of the information space–time relationship of humans to buildings, places, objects, and relationships, past, present, and future (see Figure 2.13).

Transmutation is a complex term given to the topological shape- and capability-changing characteristics of an environment. Emerging new technologies will continue to change the boundaries of physical domains and social and societal connectivity. They enable the ability to do things through information assets and solutions that can alter human experience.

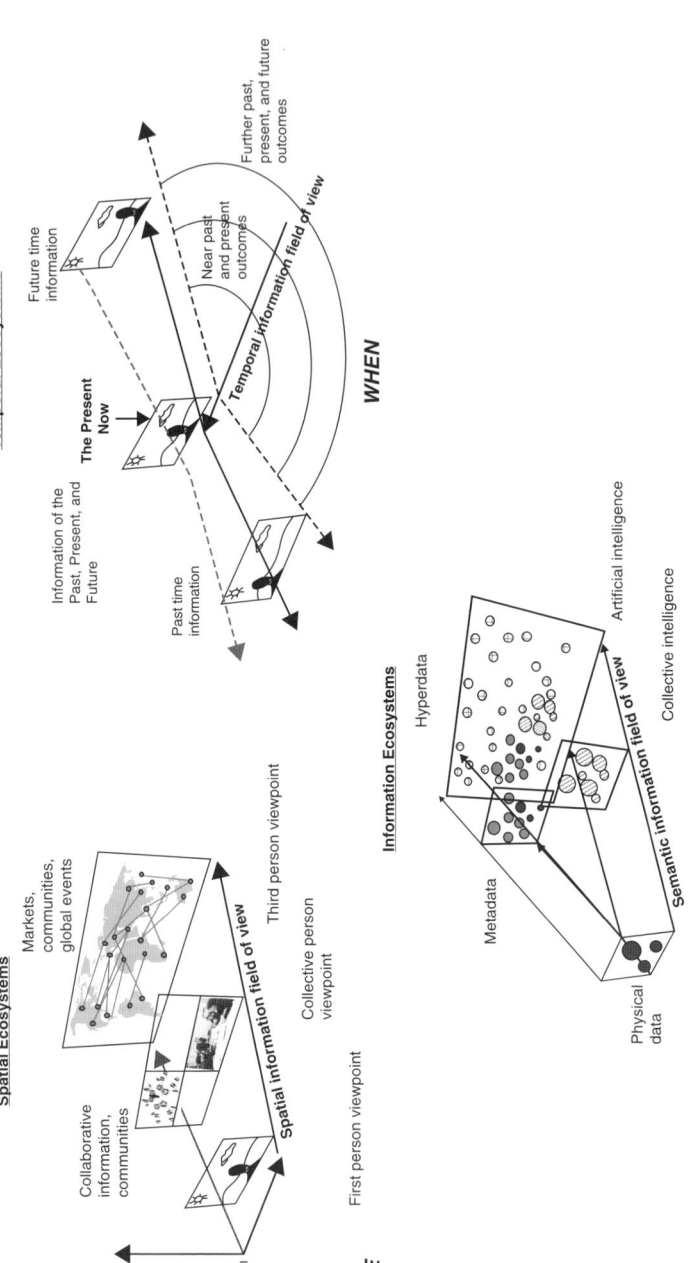

Temporal Ecosystems

Future time information

Further past, present, and future outcomes

Near past and present outcomes

Temporal information field of view

WHEN

The Present Now

Information of the Past, Present, and Future

Past time information

Spatial Ecosystems

Markets, communities, global events

Third person viewpoint

Collective person viewpoint

Spatial information field of view

Collaborative information, communities

First person viewpoint

Immediate sensory information

WHERE

Information Ecosystems

Hyperdata

Artificial intelligence

Collective intelligence

Semantic information field of view

Augmented intelligence

Metadata

Physical data

WHAT

FIGURE 2.13 Convergence of digitization in physical and virtual space and time

Transformation of Physical Workplaces to Virtual Workspaces by Digitization

These concepts of spatial, temporal, and semantic context are important ideas in enabling understanding of what it means to think digitally.

Digital workspaces are areas within the digital ecosystem that define *specific points of reference* for how the digital technologies and information are brought together in a specific context.

Digital workspaces are implementations of PEC models representing space–time STC model interactions.

Digital workspaces are the building blocks of the digital enterprise (see Figure 2.14).

The term *digital workspace* is a useful "unit" to consider in the definition of digital design. We will explore a number of digital workspaces that provide patterns that can be observed in the digital ecosystem and digital enterprises.

> Digital workspace
> - Digital workspace is defined by physical and virtual data and objects associated with that domain workspace, which can work collectively for the ecosystem and enterprise
> - Digital workspaces span physical, extended, and contextual areas of an ecosystem (PEC)
> - Each digital workspace is defined by spatial–temporal characteristics to enable its context (STC)

Definition of Digital Workspaces from an Ecosystem Perspective

If we step back and look at the bigger picture of the ecosystem, the physical world can be thought of as representing the total environment that we live in today. Yet in the virtual sense through the information era this

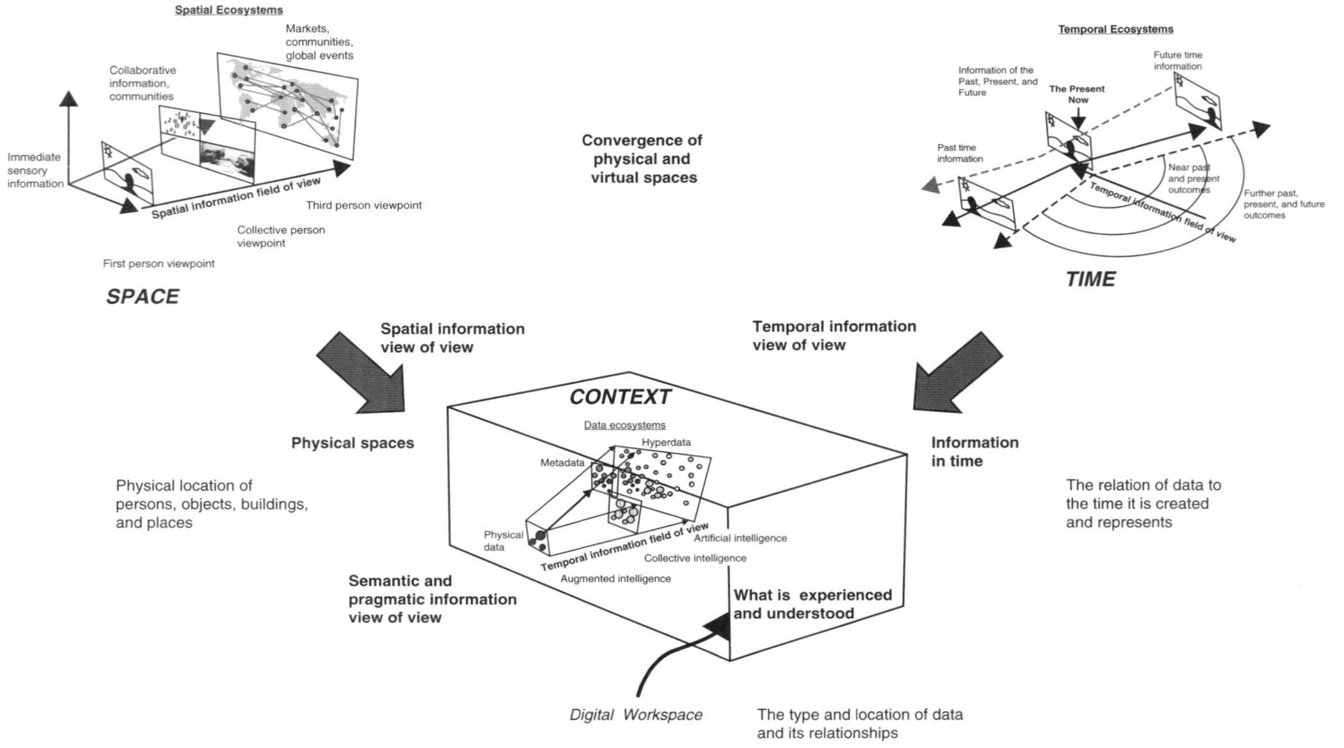

Spatial Ecosystems

Markets, communities, global events

Third person viewpoint

Spatial information field of view

Collective person viewpoint

Collaborative information, communities

First person viewpoint

Immediate sensory information

SPACE

Temporal Ecosystems

Future time information

Further past, present, and future outcomes

Near past and present outcomes

Temporal information field of view

The Present Now

Information of the Past, Present, and Future

Past time information

TIME

The relation of data to the time it is created and represents

Convergence of physical and virtual spaces

Temporal information view of view

Information in time

Spatial information view of view

Physical spaces

Semantic and pragmatic information view of view

CONTEXT

Data ecosystems

Hyperdata

Artificial intelligence

Collective intelligence

Temporal information field of view

Augmented intelligence

Metadata

Physical data

What is experienced and understood

Digital Workspace

The type and location of data and its relationships

Physical location of persons, objects, buildings, and places

FIGURE 2.14 Digital workspace

has become increasingly interconnected. Telecommunications, devices, and sensors grow across the physical world and enable a kind of virtual representation of this in digital maps and shared media content from potentially anywhere on earth. The virtual work does not constrain the geographical and physical limitations of the locations but can represent many views, of "worlds," depending on what information and context is being considered.

Indeed, in the physical world there are many types of ecosystems that might be described as systems in their own right. These ecosystems can be considered as different viewpoints of the same overall ecosystem. Examples of these include societal ecosystems that have formed over millennia in villages, towns, and cities across countries and continents. Commercial ecosystems have spawned in trading products and services in market sectors from agriculture to mining, manufacturing, and service industries, having grown with populations and driven economic ecosystems for wealth creation and wellbeing.

The modern exploration of ecosystems is of course not earthbound, and this discussion can now include the low earth orbit International Space Station (ISS) and satellite technology. Space exploration now extends to other planets and the Deep Space Network (DSN) is an examples of the ambition to reach further. The technological ecosystems are entangled across these ecosystems enabling the potential of new digital workspaces that connect different experiences and resources.

Definition of Digital Workspaces from a Human Perspective

The definition of physical workplaces as virtual workspaces can be based on a number of practical physical considerations. We can break this down into the immediate human space of reference in considering three types:

- **Physical spaces** that humans live and work in
- **Transit spaces** that humans travel and move between
- **Biological spaces** that represent the human body condition and living habitat

Digitization of these spaces creates new virtual workspaces that can change how the physical workplaces function and interact with the human experience.

Physical workplaces

These are the contemporary locations, streets, sidewalks, buildings, rooms, and other physical objects that are the small and larger scale artifacts of the physical world. Consumable items such as food, money, clothes, and other temporary objects can all be seen as the things that are present in the living workspace.

Virtual physical workspace

A virtual space of a physical location is the enablement of the physical space with digital technologies such as "smart wall," which can display content or offer touch-sensitive interactivity. Physical locations can be connected: for example, in a web teleconference remote locations can be shared as if they were in the same physical location.

Transit workplaces

Objects are not just static: cars, planes, and trains move. They are the same as fixed artifacts except that they have an additional property, which is that they move.

Virtual transit workspaces

The connected car is an example of a transit space that may have GPS and other remote connectivity to provide information and entertainment while on the move.

Biological workplaces

The human body has many biological subsystems. The organs, the respiratory, nervous, muscular, skeletal, and many other systems represent the biological "systems platform". The human body also has emotional, intellectual, spiritual, and cultural essence of being. Biological systems can be treated as another "space" that are manifest in the real physical world. The social collectiveness of groups, communities, and organizations also represent a kind of biological living space.

Biological living systems can be taken to include the ecological environment we live in: animals, insects, plants, rivers, forests, land, sea, atmosphere, and the biosphere that encompasses the planet.

Virtual biological workspaces

At human body level, the use of implants to augment organs and monitor health, such as heart pacemakers to artificial limbs to microchip implants. Wearable technology can externally augment human health and fashion and lifestyle accessories are seen in eyewear, wrist bands, and smart clothing. Advances in organ regeneration and genetic engineering suggest new frontiers for augmented human medical lifestyles and conditions.

Design of Digital Workspaces

Digital workspaces, as we have seen, are connected spaces in a digital ecosystem.

The physical enterprise is a commercial organization that can be constructed from the physical, transitional, and human spaces; the physical objects, rooms, and buildings of the enterprise, and the transport and traffic networks between the organization and its markets; the human capital and skills that represent the enterprise and its partners and customers.

There are potentially many digital workspaces that can be formed from the digitization of these physical, transit, and biological spaces.

We will focus on six major patterns of digital workspaces in a digital enterprise (see Figure 2.15):

• Object workspace
• Room and facility workspace

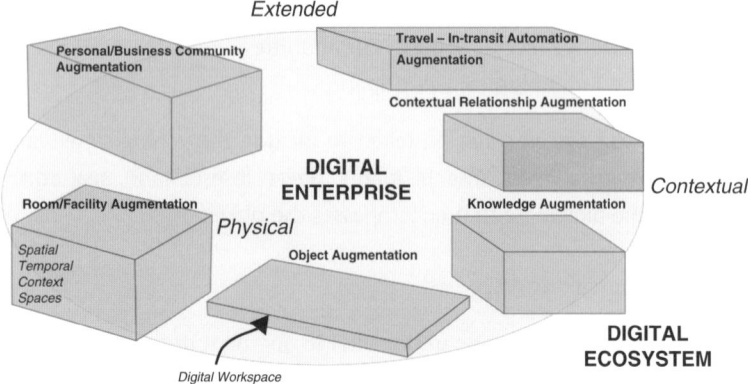

FIGURE 2.15 Definition of digital workspaces

- Personal workspace and business community workspace
- Travel and transition workspace
- Contextual relationship workspace
- Knowledge workspace

Definitions of digital workspaces

Object workspace

An entity that can be defined by content and function. Objects can be materially physical such as a chair, cup, or a wall, or virtual digital objects such as music or a digital book. Objects can be non-living and living.

Examples of PEC model object workspace - physical objects in a kitchen, such as cooker, plates, forks, cups, food items, drink items, fridge, kettle.

Examples of STC model object workspace – information on recipes or fridge reordering can be virtually connected to digital services; virtual objects can be used, such as 3D printing of objects.

Room and facility workspace

The physical walls, floors, and objects within a room; a building made up of rooms and floors. Rooms and facilities can be privately owned or public place facilities such as municipal services, parks, swimming pools, and libraries. Rooms and buildings can also be virtual if connected remotely to other rooms and buildings as a connected virtual workspace, for example a simultaneous webcast of a concert or a theatre event for a viewing audience community.

Examples of PEC model room/facility workspace – living room spaces, corridors, the building structure; the collection of buildings in a shopping mall; a factory complex; collections of facilities that are managed as a unit.

Examples of STC model room/facility workspace – visualization screens mounted on walls to display information; the air conditioning system and heating control system for automated room ambient environment control.

Personal workspace and business community workspace

The personal private and public set of information connected for individuals or a collection of individuals. This may include a commercial relationship that represents a business trading community.

A human body can be regarded as a collection of systems, a community as it were of subsystems that together function as a human body.

Example of PEC model personal and business community workspace – a personal set of social connections; a business trading community in a supply chain network; a set of buildings and business units that represent a city community space.

Example of STC model personal and business community workspace – wearable technology to monitor wellbeing for medical research; collecting information across a community of patients; a social network of personal friends or a marketplace of consumers and sellers.

Travel and transition workspace

Whereas rooms and facilities may be considered as fixed, physically non-moving assets, other assets such as vehicles and transportation network infrastructure such as roads, railways, shipping ports, and airports represent a combination of facilities and moving transit spaces. These physically movable spaces may also be digitized and follow the human user and connectivity as they physically move from one location to another.

Example of PEC model travel and transitional workspace – a personal set of social connections; a business trading community in a supply chain network.

Example of STC model travel and transitional workspace – logistics package real-time tracking; connected car on-board driver assistance and infotainment system.

Contextual relationship workspace

A contextual workspace where the products and services are specifically tailored to the needs of the situation at that time and location. Context workspaces have a feedback loop that collects information, analyzes, and then makes decisions and feedbacks to the context of the situation. Context workspaces can be passive or active in the way they collect and feed back a specific response to a situation. Passive, being not visual or perceived by the human, and active, involving the human user who is aware of the context action.

Example of PEC model contextual workspace – a set of food produce displayed by category in a shop; a book section in a physical library offering genres; a concierge service at a hotel reception desk; an information point in a city center.

Example of STC model contextual workspace – an online book recommendations service; a GPS satellite navigation planner using real-time road traffic adjustments; a body health feedback sensor providing real-time alerts on movement exercise; an automated alarm system for intruder alert that may notify authorities automatically through geolocation monitoring and alerts; an interactive art display that has touch sensors to activate different displays.

Knowledge workspace

The information about an object, place, or person that provides awareness and insight into the condition and nature of the objects and locations.

Example of PEC model knowledge workspace – information manuals on use of TV devices for channel and services selection setup; a set of photographs about a location stored on a digital map service; aregister of attendees for a concert or music event; an engineering design schematic drawing.

Example of STC model knowledge workspace – a digital brand with associated products and social media activity about the brand; a set of shared wiki pages for collaborative knowledge sharing and employee development; a set of open source code downloads and coding development by a crowdsourced community; a set of recommendations and ratings online about a restaurant.

Together these workspaces represent a combination of many different types of digitization experiences to be found across industries and markets. The digital enterprise is a construction of these workspaces, the building out of the connected systems and physical locations in ways that create new value networks.

The digital workspace is seeing an explosion of technologies that are connected and immersed into these workspaces. This illustrates just some of the technologies that are available today in these domains. But as we saw earlier in the book, the number of objects, devices, and connections is projected to grow enormously. This is the digital ecosystem of 25 billion objects and beyond.

Digital Workspaces as Digital Platforms

A building can have objects, chairs, tables, and other artifacts, in rooms. The building may be part of a set of buildings, walkways, roads, and municipal facilities such as street lighting, traffic management, and community services that together may represent a village, town, or city. Inside the building there can be objects that themselves can connect to other objects in the same building or virtually to other objects in other buildings, thereby creating a virtual workspace across physical buildings. The buildings and the wider location and resources could connect with other cities and location services as a wider ecosystem of communities and collaborations.

These can be considered as areas in which digital workspaces can connect and build together into a set of physical and virtual services. In building our digital enterprise we describe this as constructing digital workspaces that together represent the operation of the enterprise.

Digital workspaces can be used to define how the digital enterprise is built by connecting physical spaces in the enterprise and the wider ecosystem. It supports market-making activities through the creation of digital business models that work by using these workspaces to connect physical and virtual objects, locations, and in transport between these locations.

This is the "big idea" of digitization and indicates how digital ecosystems and the digital economy will work in the future. Digital workspaces move beyond the idea of UX and CX, and begin to be constructed so that users, customers, and the enterprise work as a digital business.

Digital workspaces are digital platforms that support a multilayered set of capabilities that are specific to each enterprise. Here we list some examples of digital technologies that can be used to construct these digital workspaces (see Figure 2.16).

In the next chapter we will look at case studies of how organizations have used digital technologies to build their digital enterprise. The following examples illustrate technologies that can enable digital workspace platforms (see Tables 2.3 to 2.8)

FIGURE 2.16   Digital workspaces as platforms

TABLE 2.3   Digital knowledge platform examples

Digital Workspace Platform	Examples of Digital Technologies enabling this Digital Workspace
Knowledge augmentation Knowledge platforms	• Crowd knowledge – e.g. Wikipedia • Real-time metrics dashboard visualization • Multi-device data synchronization • Augmented communication library – context of past activity and associations • Live personal profile, lookup Bio image search and knowledge access • Co-innovation • 2D and 3D design visualization • Location information support, e.g. nearest stock, person, assistance

TABLE 2.4   Digital contextual augmentation platform examples

Digital Workspace Platform	Examples of Digital Technologies Enabling this Digital Workspace
Contextual relationship augmentation Contextual Platforms	• Automated identity recognition • Location/local knowledge access • Ideation, co-creation • Preference-based communication routing automation • Location information support, e.g. nearest stock, person, assistance • Location information support, e.g. Nearest stock, person, assistance • Integrated work and user/device • Knowledge augmentation "did you know... ?"

TABLE 2.5   Digital transit platform examples

Digital Workspace Platform	Examples of Digital Technologies Enabling this Digital Workspace
Travel - In transit automation Travel-Transit Platforms	• Travel platforms • Package transit tracking, transport management platforms • Workflow management • Transport event feeds • Real-time performance management • Smart connected transport scheduling • Intelligent vehicle sensors • Inter-network seamless identity management • Real-time sourcing/supply chain integration • Internetwork integration, e.g. wireless and Bluetooth

TABLE 2.6   Digital personal/business community platform examples

Digital Workspace Platform	Examples of Digital Technologies Enabling this Digital Workspace
Personal/Business Community Personal Platform Community Platform	• Personal platforms • Community platforms • Smart city energy grid • Community information grids • Real-time office/location activity • Voice commands • Physical projection to multi-user eye synchronization, auto zoom in/out, and location • Real-time voice language translation • Real-time living space ambient living • Smart room – object environment integration • Internetwork automated transfer • Information personalization, own viewpoint • Bio signature scanning • Furniture space sharing • Smart energy management • Integrated real-time diary-work scheduler • Real-time multi-party work orchestration • Crowdsource – ideation

TABLE 2.7   Digital room/facility platform examples

Digital Workspace Platform	Examples of Digital Technologies Enabling this Digital Workspace
Room/Facility Augmentation Room/Facility Platforms	• Room platforms • Facility platforms • Wall, surface gesture integration • Transparent surface projection • Virtual whiteboard • Object physical virtual animation • Solar energy, home grid • Wide angle group projection, social interaction • Spatial augmentation, virtual room • Virtual location collaboration • 3D movement sensor • 3D stereoscopic measurement and digitization • Object to Surface projection – interconnectivity – virtual model adjustment, input • Automatic proximity on/off sensing – body/location/lighting/touch • Room embedded physical sensors • Office surfaces information augmentation

TABLE 2.8   Digital object platform examples

Digital Workspace Platform	Examples of Digital Technologies Enabling this Digital Workspace
Object Augmentation Object Platforms	• Wearables, devices • Appliance/spare component specification augmentation • Low-carbon materials • Integrated object classification and semantic awareness search • Multi-purpose device – dynamic use applications in context • Flexible substrate displays on physical objects, e.g. electronic paper, smart cup • Physical/virtual object integration • Tablet/work device to virtual projection device integration • Accelerometer sensors • Physical object bio-sensing example: cup • Multi-form factor modality support • Life sciences integration • Transport/item identity specification tags • Movement three-axis gyroscope sensors • Conduction battery charging • Product cluster information • CMB contact memory buttons • NFC, QR, RFID tags

The Next Technological Era

The development of digital workspaces is part of a continuing evolution of technology over the past decades. The earlier ideas of technology and internet network-centric connectivity created a human-centric technology vision. Information could pass between the "four walls" of the organization to external entities and social networks.

But in a mere decade or less, this era is now long past: we have an explosion of digital data and connectivity with mobile devices and sensors that is ushering in a new technological era of immersive connected spaces. The early innocence of the information economy has given way to a new reality that promises new forms of digital intelligence. The human is no longer the center of the digital universe. Devices, sensors, and smart machines play a role in creating a multiplicity of physical and digital experiences that we are only just starting to see the possibilities of. Our challenge is that we make these systems what they are, and must direct their development for the benefit of society and social and economic and sustainability.

In Chapter 3 we will explore the reality of the digital enterprise today through case study examples as we pass on this journey to the next technological era. We will seek a definition of what it means to define a digital enterprise, and the lessons needed in order to create successful architecture for a digital enterprise.

Chapter Summary

In this chapter we have considered some of the basic academic foundations of modern information theory in its construction of semantic meaning and the contextual use of information from simple to complex meaning. The journey of the practitioner in the real world has evolved as the technologies available to develop new software and hardware capabilities constantly change. This will continually challenge the practitioner and the research theorist to keep up with the rate of change and make sense of the new opportunities and potential threats they may bring.

part II

Designing the Digital Enterprise

3
Design Practices in the Digital Enterprise

Chapter Introduction

We have seen case studies of enterprises that have constructed digital solutions. In this chapter we will explore how digital models can be developed using enterprise architecture modeling tools and techniques.

In this chapter we will cover:

- Example of a business model and a digital business model
- Modeling digital solutions in enterprise architecture
- Architecting digital workspace examples
- Design practices in digital enterprise
- Modular scaling design
- Ecosystem architecture

Example of a Digital Business Model Using Digital Workspaces

Introduction

The modern hospitality industry has grown since the 19th century, when only the rich and famous had free time and money to spend. As industrialization began to emerge it gave rise to mass employment, workplace automation, and by the 20th century to statutory employment rights for workers to vacation and free time. The hospitality industry has therefore been a barometer of economic activity. Private lodgings, professional hotels, restaurants, public houses, wine bars, guest rooms, and many related services from catering to building maintenance and cleaning, have created jobs and indeed a whole industry.

The hospitality industry is not restricted to leisure time, and today is integrated into the commercial activity of commuters and travel, being the "glue" for a mobile workforce. This emerging role has widened, enabling hospitality services often to represent the cultural expression of cities and countries as they seek to promote tourism and their "brand" to a local, regional, and global audience. Indeed, with national sporting events, festivals, arts, music, historical attractions, and environmental sightseeing, these have become part of a wider ecosystem that encompasses national identity and a social and cultural expression of quality of life.

In looking at the hospitality sector, therefore, it is also necessary to consider its relationship to other industries such as tourism, which was recently reported by the World Travel and Tourism Council as representing 3 percent of global GDP.[1] In reality, though, across the many industries that hospitality supports, such as distribution, transport, and other activities, it can more correctly be described as driving directly and indirectly almost 9 percent of GDP globally, generating one in ten of all jobs.

Hospitality has grown into a multi-service phenomenon that has moved beyond the basic concept of a room and a place to sleep and now includes many integrated services, such as travel, tourism, and corporate events. Private and public automobile travel, road systems, buses, rail and air travel connecting to town and city hubs that are supported by hotels and other service industry facilities all enable the economies of those regions. Tourism has increasingly segmented to support many different customer lifestyles, from family holidays to specialist explorer vacations, which in turn have driven different types of hotel and hospitality services. The development of corporate hospitality has become a significant sector in its own right, with business events and trade shows a significant growth area for hospitality services. As a result, the perception of the customer as a visitor has radically changed from the early days of leisure, and today people may use hospitality in their employment or in their free time.

Hospitality is very much associated with the psychology of human experience. Indeed, the design and management of modern hospitality services seek to create a fundamental connection to human aspirations and lifestyle, in what is termed the "needs and wants of the customer guest." The "customer experience" is consequently at the very core of hospitality, defined in the *Oxford English Dictionary* as "the friendly and generous reception and entertainment of guests, visitors, or strangers," This experience involves empathy and a personalization that reaches many different aspects of the customer journey to and from a hotel or restaurant, the experience of the visit itself, and the many associated services surrounding the location and its context, as well as the initial reason for the customer's visit. The key is in understanding the customer experience outcomes and the hospitality operational performance outcomes that support customers (see Table 3.1).

Geraldine Calpin, senior vice-president and global head of digital at Hilton Worldwide, described this as "start with the dream, people have dreams and how can we enable this to become a reality with our hospitality." It's a wonderful aspirational take on the whole concept of customer touchpoints and a good example of the hospitality role, which makes the customer the core of service excellence. Not surprisingly this is also reflected in the stated Hilton corporate vision: "To fill the earth with the light and warmth of hospitality."

TABLE 3.1   Hospitality operational versus customer outcomes

Hospitality Operational Outcomes	Customer Outcomes
• Volume of tourists and visitor traffic	• Lifestyle aspirations
• Visitor spend	• Enjoyment
• Service efficiency	• Convenience
• Personalization and guest privacy	• Employment
• Return visits	• Cultural identity

Hilton International is an American global hospitality company with a turnover of $9,735 billion in 2013. It encompasses 4,200 hotels with over 690,000 rooms in 93 countries. Hilton own, manage, and franchise 11 brands with 168,000 direct employees and 162,000 franchise employees.[2] Hilton continues to expand its hospitality assets with a further development pipeline of 1,230 hotels, consisting of approximately 210,000 rooms reported in the second quarter SEC filing in 2014.[3] It was reported in the second quarter of 2014 that Hilton has a successful loyalty card service with over 40 million HHonors™ members worldwide.

Digital hospitality leadership

Given the evolving connection of customer service and the extended definition of hospitality to take in adjacent industries, how have digital technologies been used to enable better hospitality?

Calpin explains that Hilton International has already established digital solutions to enhance the hospitality experience and is working on new areas in its future plans: "We see digital as essential to enabling hospitality. In developing our digital strategy we look at it through every stage of the customer journey. Our start point is the customer guest journey, this is where people start to dream, then they plan, they shop, then they book. Then they get ready to fly, to travel, then they arrive, then they leave, they depart by a check-out. The last part is they share, which may include social media and other forms to describe their experiences." Indeed, this idea of sharing to drive brand and service is in the Hilton loyalty scheme HHonors™ messaging: "Experiences worth sharing." "What Hilton is seeking to do with digital is to understand how it can enable, improve and enhance the guest experience and support the revenues at every point in that guest journey." "Traditionally this has been through web sites, mobile sites, and apps that create the booking capability and seeing it as the booking channel. The reality is that mobile and digital has changed how things work. I describe it as *the mobile phone is people's remote control to the world.*" "The digital solutions need to be designed around mobile and how it can be used to turn the customer experience into the journey with this in mind." Calpin illustrates this point with an example of a customer who looks at the video of one of the Hilton hotels in Hawaii, then goes online to book. The website can be linked to an appropriate airline website. The day before she travels, checking in by the guest may be enabled online, providing added convenience and timesaving. There may also be online facilities to allow the guest to choose the room she wants to stay in: Hilton International have mapped 300,000 of their 600,000 rooms in the same way that airlines have seat maps for their aircraft cabins. They also have floor plans for most of their hotels, while guests are even able to use their cell phone to open their hotel room door: "In Hilton we recently announced a new service called 'Hilton Straight-to-room™' which enables the use of the mobile phone as a remote key." Calpin explains that in market research it was found that 84 percent of guests would like the option to quickly check in and to go directly to their room on arrival.[4]

The use of digital services through mobile devices and apps is enhancing the way Hilton meets its customers' needs and desires. These technologies enable a superior hospitality experience, empowering guests to select rooms, room types, and room numbers, using their mobile phones. Calpin says that in some of the Hilton brands, the Hilton mobile apps allow guests to use their phone to order room service, or request a car rental. In some hotels the same mobile app can act as a room environmental control, enabling the guest to remotely open and close the window blinds and control the room temperature. "It is about 'digital hospitality' and also about 'digital revenue' but striking the right balance, our business is all about hospitality so it is primarily about making the stay more hospitable through enabling what the guest wants to achieve these outcomes."

This is just the beginning of what digital technologies might enable in the future (see Figure 3.1). Mobile is clearly a key strategy that is a central part of delivering an enhanced customer experience for Hilton International guests. Calpin explains that Hilton is a leader in many of these areas and is planning to create even more hospitality enhancements through digital technologies. "I can envision a situation where you are brushing your teeth in one of the Hilton hotels in the morning and the mirror will light up with a call from your partner; your schedule will appear displayed underneath

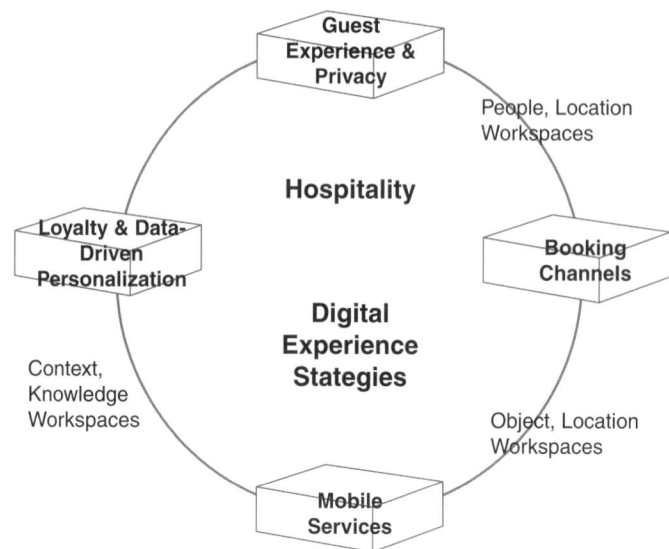

FIGURE 3.1   **Smart hospitality – digital experience strategies**

it. You are asked to pick up something on the way home and you can add it dynamically into your schedule there and then and automatically synchronize it back to your mobile phone and personal electronic diary."

These have not arrived just yet, but a more immersive environment is the great promise of digital enterprises. This theme is seen repeatedly in other case studies drawn from a range of leading companies, which continue to push the boundaries of what is possible with digital technology. The connection between how to engage a customer and the lifecycle of digital hospitality strategies has several lessons for us (see Figure 3.2).

In the area of data analytics, large amounts of information are generated in many industries. Calpin describes this as an opportunity to enhance service personalization. "The issue today is being able to measure everything and having too much data. The challenge is often identifying which of the metrics are important to measure performance of the business and the impact of digital."

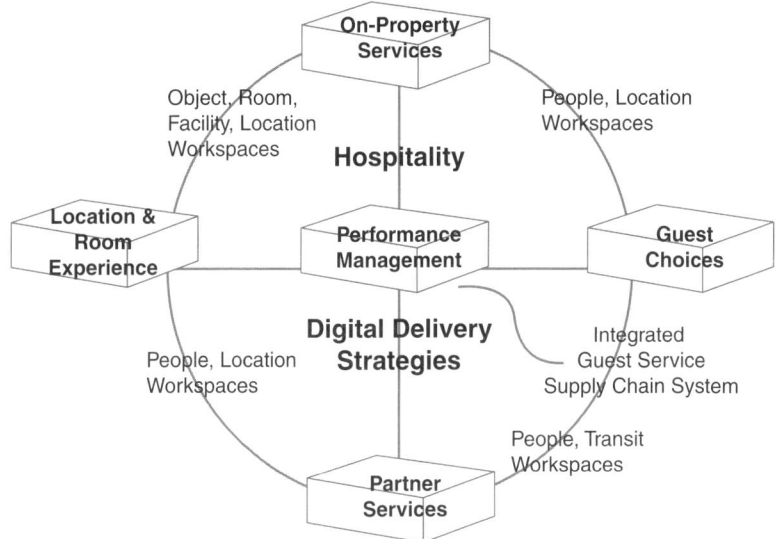

FIGURE 3.2 Smart hospitality – digital delivery strategies

Big data analytics can support the commercial side as well as the supply chain for operations and the delivery of services. Calpin explains that there are many metrics that can be used to measure guest service usage, such as the number of times they visit Hilton and partner websites and the number of bookings. All these information points enable better insight and potential service opportunities.

"The other thing digital will enable apart from making guests' lives easier is personalization with digital technologies. In the past we would use segmentation to classify customers, but now with digital you can treat every customer uniquely," Calpin explains. "When a guest arrives at a hotel, the service could be enabled to provide enhanced services through already knowing what the guest likes and what preferences are. The concierge service at the front desk in the hotel can better anticipate what the guest might need and ask about past stays and provide a more tailored service and advice to support the guest's needs. Personalization enables better hospitality and is a core aspect of the business strategy for Hilton." Calpin underpins this with the need for privacy of personal data across all channels that touch the customer. This forms part of the Hilton International Global Privacy Policy, which covers how personal information is collected and managed. It includes all aspects of the operation, including mobile and location-based services that are part of the digital and operational strategy.[5]

In the area of digital innovation Hilton have used crowdsourcing via crowd marketplace service provider companies, including Communispace and IdeaConnection, to develop new ideas for business development, feedback on product launches, websites, and other areas.[6] Calpin explains that there are also public community spaces that can provide ideas and opinion. An example is flyertalk, which is a social network website forum for frequent flyers.[7] These sites provide real-time social network chat and opinions from a range of potential and current customers, and can offer very useful reactions to current and future products and service ideas.

Performance management

Understanding how the hospitality industry works and its differences from other industries is a key point that Calpin reiterates: "Competitive differentiation is different in the hospitality business to other industries such as manufacturing or pharmaceuticals because in those industries it's more about managing the right process and supply chain distribution and maintaining it once it's in place. In hospitality no part of your business is factorized, we have to constantly monitor and deliver at every point because it is a service. We rely on people to smile and create that excellent customer experience every time they meet the guest. While it is not a low margin business, it is nevertheless a complex business to recreate this experience every time the guest arrives and in every moment they use our services. Digital technology does not cut people out of this, it provides technology to employees to enhance the service to be more efficient and effective for our guest. It helps us to know who you are, know your HHonours™ membership level and benefits, and to give a personalized service to make the total visitor experience better end to end."

Hilton have moved this concept to work up and down their supply chain of operations to establish a connected hospitality experience.

Digital system capabilities are essential in managing quality and performance across a diverse range of locations and a mix of own premises and franchise businesses. This also provides a useful lesson in best practice that underpins Hilton International's business model and global brand operation, which is built on people and the hospitality they deliver.

The hospitality industry in the 21st century has become part of the global economy, and today represents an important part of the integrated services ecosystem. The use of digital technologies has and will continue to create significant opportunities for new digital enterprises.

Modeling Digital Solutions in Enterprise Architecture

In the design of enterprise architecture we can develop digital enterprises by using a modeling notation such as ArchiMate, an open and independent modeling notation for enterprise architecture from The Open Group, an internationally recognized standards body.

There is a good explanation of the ArchiMate® language in the *White Paper ArchiMate® 2.0 – Understanding the Basics* (see Figure 3.3).

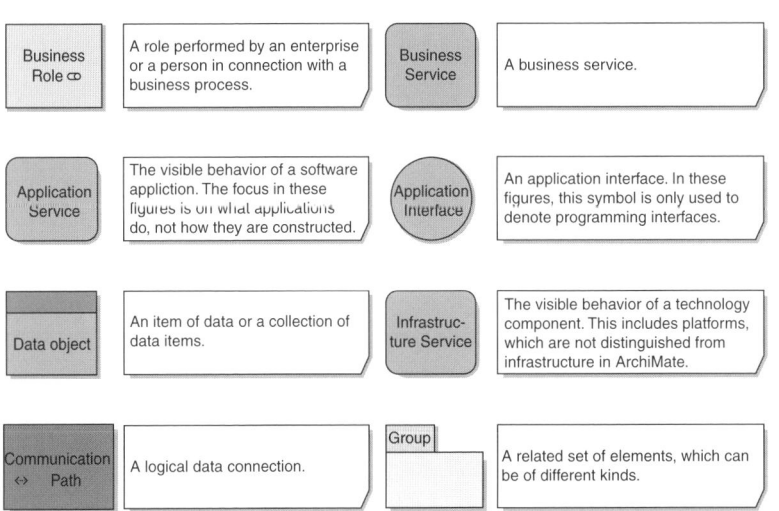

FIGURE 3.3 ArchiMate® notations symbol examples (copyright The Open Group)

Practitioners in enterprise architecture will typically define a technical reference model that describes the layers of an application architecture, one of the oldest concepts in computing. The Open Group provides a good example of this in Figure 3.4.[8,9]

Figure 3.5 is an example of an ArchiMate model that represents the same concept using selected symbols from the ArchiMate modeling notation.

This representation has four layers that characterize the essential human and machine physical components.

- **Role** – the human actor or machine actor that is the user interaction of the technology
- **Application** – the software function and digital content that represent the digital service used by the role

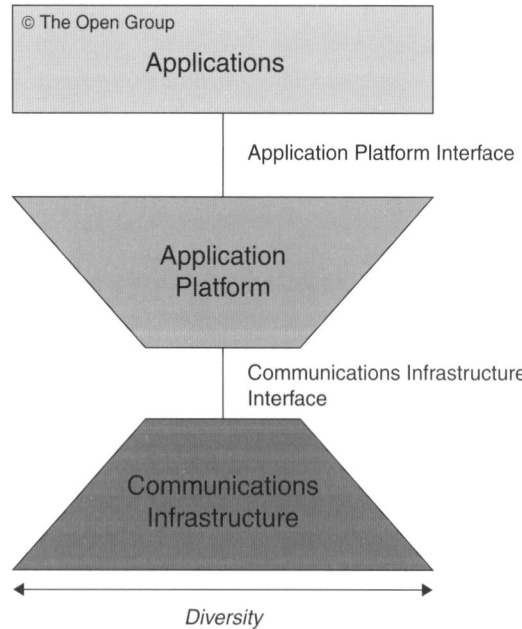

FIGURE 3.4   Technical reference model concept (copyright The Open Group)

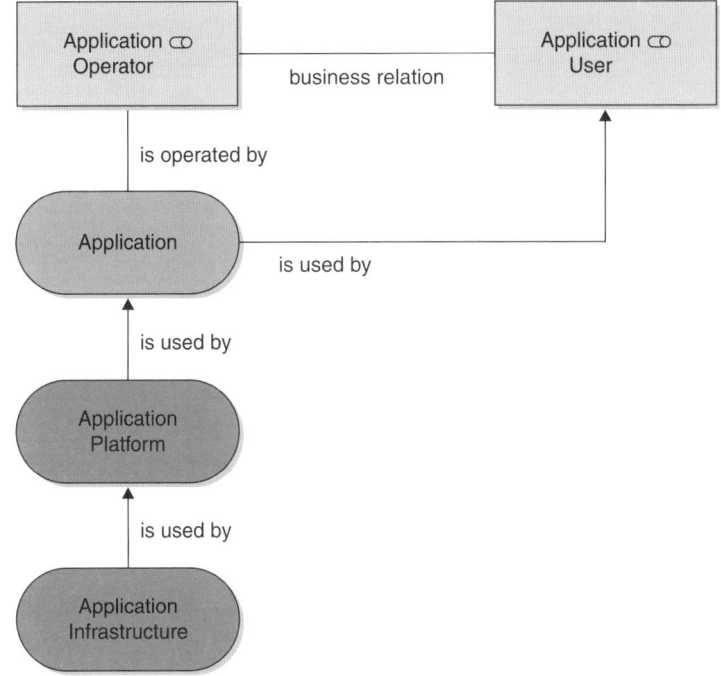

FIGURE 3.5 ArchiMate® example of the technical reference model for an application model (copyright The Open Group)

- **Application platform** – the operating platform that supports the application and content used by the role
- **Communications infrastructure** – the internetwork structure that carries the local and remote content and service

We will use this basic notation in our examples of a digital workspaces design and digital enterprise model.

A second feature we need to show is how the combinations of roles and digital technologies are combined to create a business process flow, a key activity of a business model. This will be done by using business process "swim lanes" to describe the use of digital technologies in selected digital business model examples (see Figure 3.6). The technology layers model defines a general arrangement of enterprise architecture encompassing applications, platform,

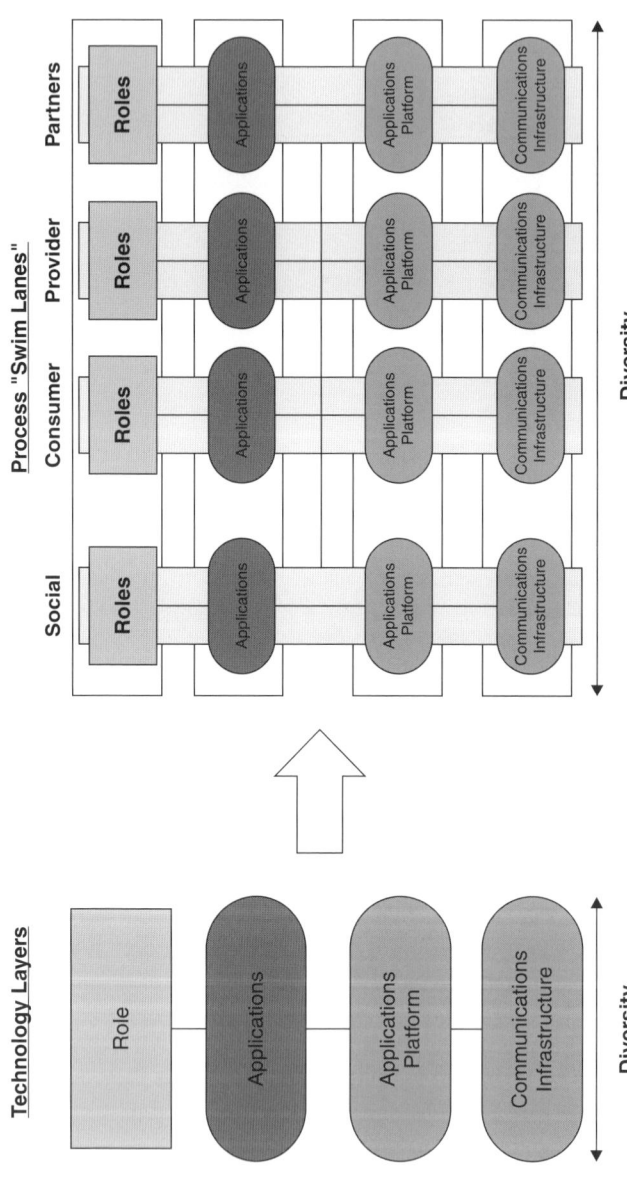

FIGURE 3.6 Enterprise architecture basic framework

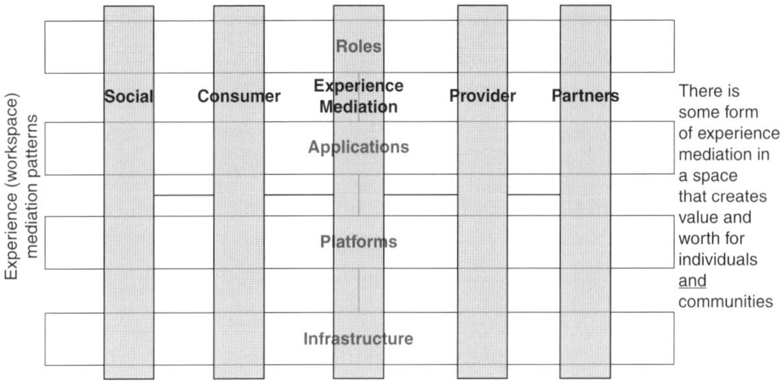

The figure shows a swim-lane matrix. Along the left vertical axis: Experience (workspace) mediation patterns. Columns across the top: Roles — Social, Consumer, Experience Mediation, Provider, Partners. Horizontal bands: Applications, Platforms, Infrastructure. On the right side a note reads: "There is some form of experience mediation in a space that creates value and worth for individuals and communities"

FIGURE 3.7 / Experience mediation role example

and infrastructure.[10] For example, a mobile application may run on a mobile device operating system that acts as a platform for the software and content that is delivered to the role user. The communications infrastructure is the mobile device connectivity that may be used to transmit and receive data. In enterprise systems and the wider marketplace there are many roles involved, so we use the process swim lanes as a general modeling framework to illustrate multiple user roles, devices, applications, and various platforms and infrastructure that may come into play for a specific digital solution or enterprise situation.

In the process swim lanes framework we can add a further role called "Experience mediation", which may be used in some of the digital business model examples (see Figure 3.7). This illustrates how the digital workspaces are created to enable different kinds of user and customer experience. We will see many examples of these in the digital business models created by digital technologies.

Architecting a Digital Workspace Example

Let us now explore an example of the digital business model using this modeling notation.

We use the business process swim lane framework to develop examples of digital technologies in selected digital business models. This example is part of a hotel hospitality service that uses digital technologies to create a "connected guest experience." We will explore this in more detail later in the chapter, but highlight here the key features we are capturing in the framework model that is used. We have four different digital services:

1. A mobile app guest service for inquiries about hotel facilities and guest bookings
2. A mobile apps marketplace for partner services related to the guest stay and hotel
3. A guest arrival service that includes check-in, room configuration, and booking service
4. A guest onward journey departure service that includes check-out and onward travel planning

The following process model illustrates the concept we will use in the ArchiMate modeling notation combining the technology layers and these four digital services (see Figure 3.8).

The model also shows the digital platforms that may be built in support of these digital services and user experiences.

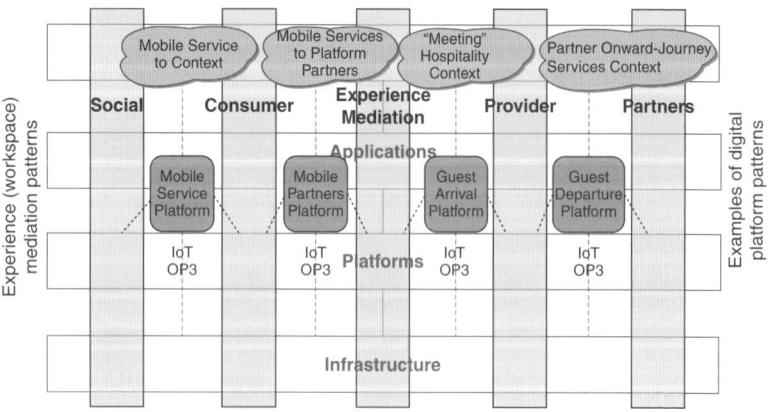

FIGURE 3.8   **Example of connected guest digital workspace**

This is a conceptual view of the architecture; the specific physical implementation will define the digital platforms that are used to support these services. In Figure 3.8 we have four platforms: a mobile services platform, a mobile partner apps platform, a guest arrival platform, and a guest departure platform. In the example here, we use an "IoT OP3" notation to depict the platform standard as an Internet of Things, Open Platform 3 type of open digital service.[11] This could also be a public cloud platform, a managed/hosted private data center platform, or an appliance installed physically on site.

The aim is to illustrate that the design of a digital workspace in an enterprise can encompass roles, services, and platforms that may be physically inside or outside the enterprise organization (or both). The digital platforms in this example could be inside the digital enterprise or hosted outside as a service that is used by the digital enterprise. For example, the guest arrival and guest departure platforms could be one integrated platform owned by the hotel business. This would be an Internet of Things platform connecting hotel room sensors and services for guests to use on arrival. This platform could also host a B2C or B2B platform and its associated community of customers and providers.

Our objective is to create a digital workspace for the hotel hospitality enterprise, an eHotel-connected guest experience. By bringing these together we can start to visualize the digital workspace illustrated in Figure 3.9.

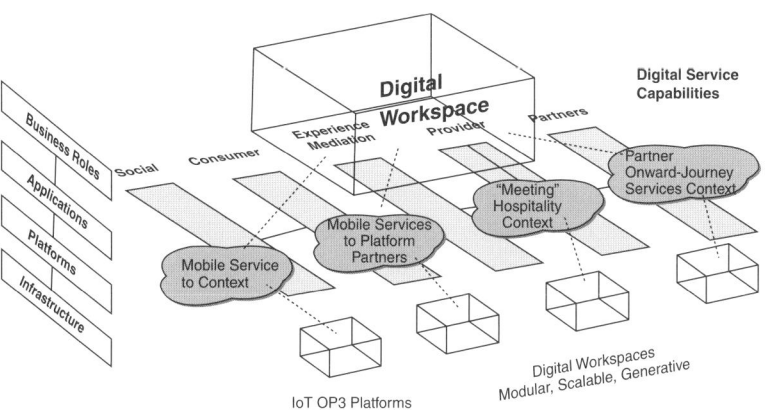

FIGURE 3.9 Modular, scalable, generative digital workspace

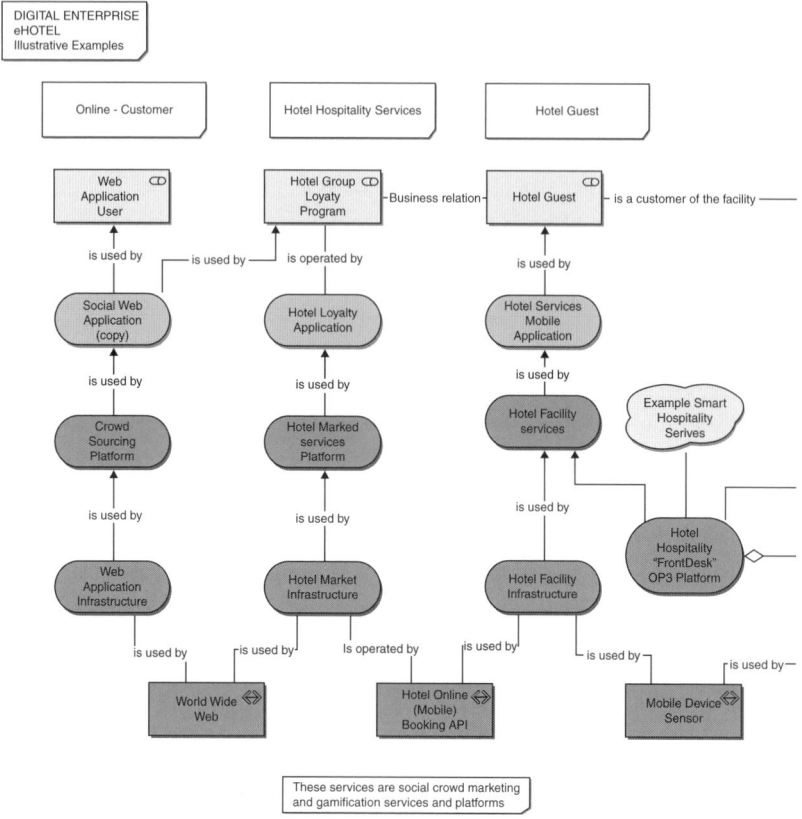

FIGURE 3.10 An eHotel digital enterprise architecture model example

A digital business model for the connected hospitality experience enables a hotel enterprise to develop a set of connected digital workspaces that can "follow" the guest through their visit lifecycle before, during, and after their stay. In this way, a more contextual, personalized set of digital services is constructed that enables guests, hotel staff, and service partners to better connect with each other and optimize each others' experience and product service offerings.

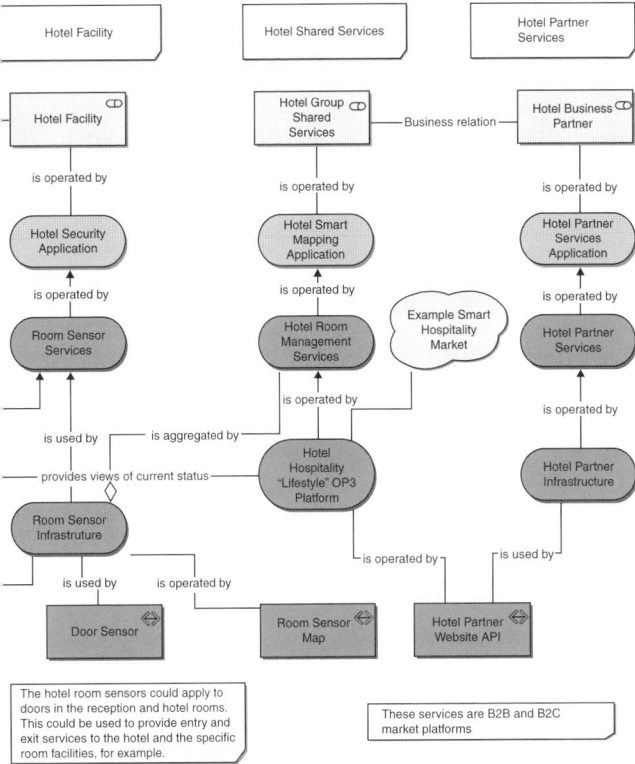

These digital workspaces can represent the whole hotel or just parts of the organization. The aim is that each digital service is scalable and modular, thereby fitting specific guest needs and able to generate monetizable value as well as good guest experience.

Here are some examples of digital enterprise architectures using the notation we previously described. The models are rendered using the open architecture tool ArchiMate.

Example 1 – Digital Hospitality Enterprise Architecture Model

Figure 3.10 is a *conceptual* architecture illustration of the eHotel digital services we described in the previous section. In the example there are two digital services platforms:

- Hotel hospitality "front desk" IoT platform for checking in and hotel room configuration and mobile app services.
- Hotel hospitality "lifestyle" platform to provide hotel room services and hotel partner services during the stay and onward journey support.

The following are more examples of conceptual architecture models that are explored in the detailed case studies.

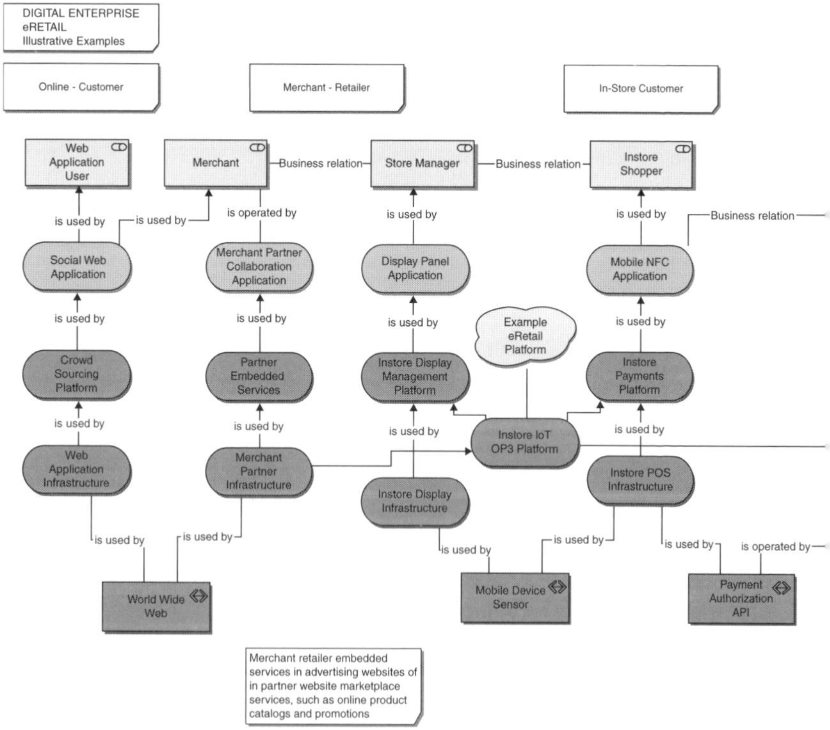

FIGURE 3.11 An eRetail digital enterprise architecture model example

Example 2 – Digital Retail Enterprise Architecture Model

An eRetail set of digital services. The digital enterprise model example shows three digital services examples (see Figure 3.11):

- In-store IoT platform for connecting in-store advertising and information display monitors to mobile apps in shoppers' smartphones.
- Online electronic payments platform providing digital payments processing by the payment issuer. The platform could be used to develop further issuer services to merchants and payment customers based on data usage profile.
- VMI (Vendor Managed Inventory) platform that supports connected services.

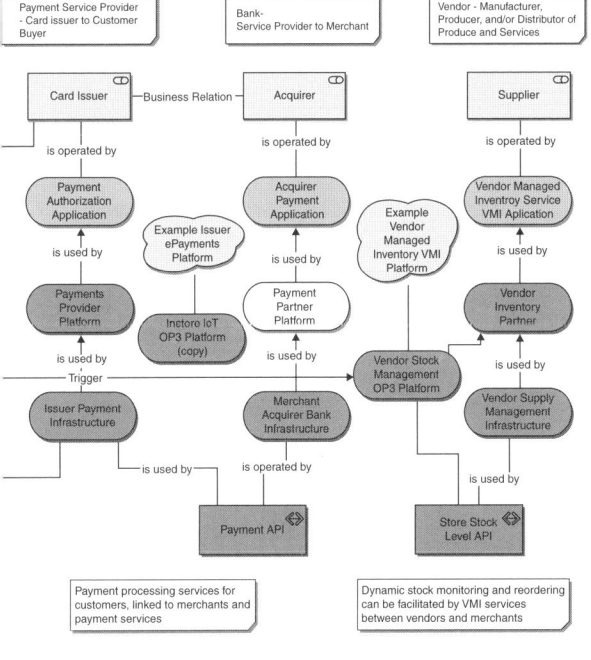

Example 3 – Connected Car Digital Enterprise Architecture Model

A connected car set of digital services. The digital enterprise model spans connectivity between the vehicle driver, owner to distributor, and back to the original vehicle manufacturer and component suppliers (see Figure 3.12).

- On-board vehicle sensor automation platform to support in-car services that can include GRP, mobile app integration, information and entertainment services, and other productivity- and service-related

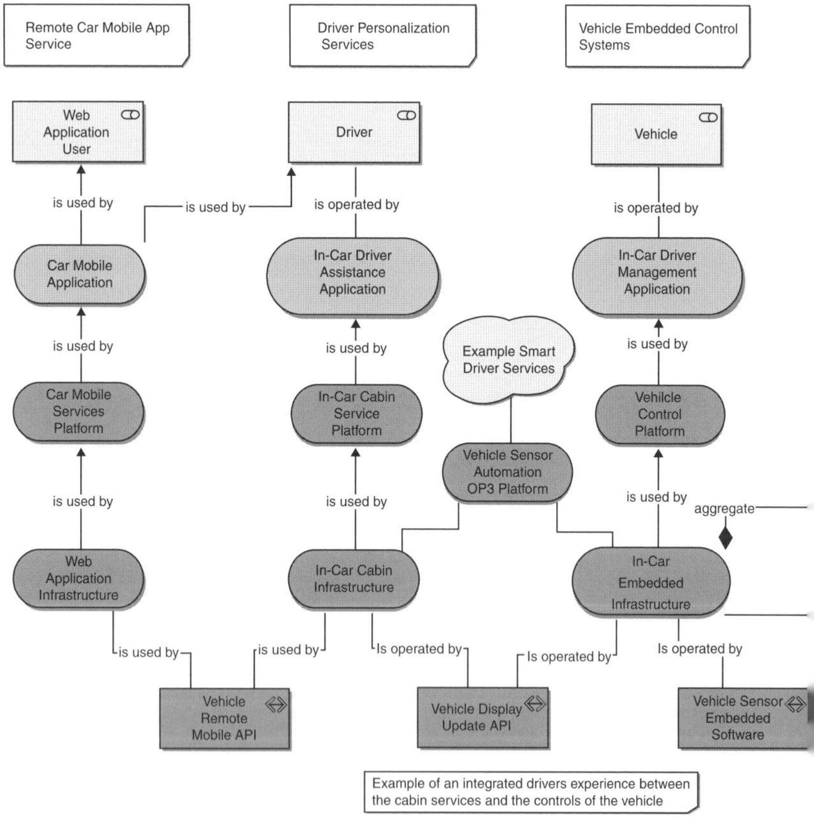

```
Remote Car Mobile App          Driver Personalization        Vehicle Embedded Control
Service                        Services                      Systems

   Web                              Driver                       Vehicle
   Application
   User

   is used by      ─is used by─   is operated by            is operated by

   Car Mobile                    In-Car Driver                In-Car Driver
   Application                   Assistance                   Management
                                 Application                  Application

   is used by                    is used by    Example Smart   is used by
                                               Driver Services

   Car Mobile                    In-Car Cabin                  Vehilcle
   Services                      Service                       Control
   Platform                      Platform                      Platform

                                               Vehicle Sensor
                                               Automation
   is used by                    is used by    OP3 Platform    is used by
                                                                          aggregate─
   Web                           In-Car Cabin                  In-Car
   Application                   Infrastructure                Embedded
   Infrastructure                                              Infrastructure

   ─is used by─   ┌is used by┘   └Is operated by┐  ┌Is operated by┘   Is operated by

           Vehicle                    Vehicle Display           Vehicle Sensor
           Remote                     Update API                Embedded
           Mobile API                                           Software

                                Example of an integrated drivers experience between
                                the cabin services and the controls of the vehicle
```

FIGURE 3.12 A connected car digital enterprise architecture example

functions. The platform may also be embedded sensors in the car that monitor vehicle control and maintenance tasks for oil, gas, tire pressure, and other engineering functions.

• Vehicle usage data collection platform for connected remote services to car manufacturer design and service management. This may be used for remote vehicle analysis, providing translation research data for next-generation vehicle design.

• Vehicle product lifecycle management to coordinate vehicle manufacturer and suppliers' ecosystems to manage parts and product development. Data and application code may be upgraded remotely back into

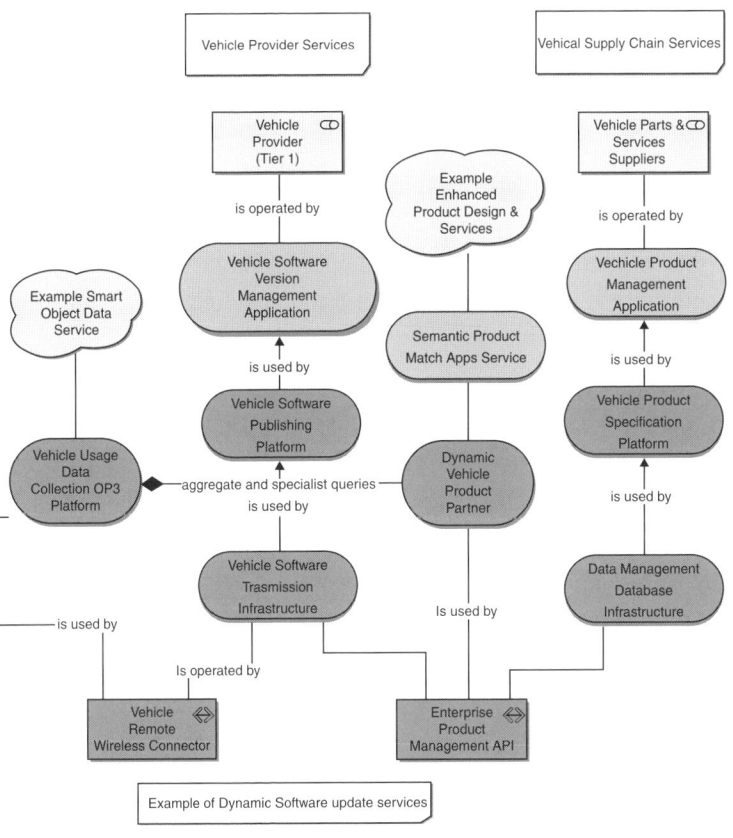

the vehicle, providing in-service vehicle improvements and additional driver, owner, and distribution services.

Design Practices in Digital Enterprise

From our exploration of building a digital enterprise, with case studies and in-depth digital business models, there are several concluding observations for practitioners.

- Modular scalable multi-sided platforms
- Competition moving to the ecosystem level
- The rise of digital ecosystem architecture
- The future of intelligence workspaces
- Digital workspace pattern catalog

Modular Scalable Multi-Sided Platforms

We have seen in these examples of digital business models that building a digital enterprise involves creating digital technology solutions that can support scalability through a "modular architecture" and a clear view of "digital platforming."

This is a common theme that runs through all the case studies and practitioners' lessons. Modularity is evident in the digital content, devices, and application services, which can be a collection of networked devices, social network communities, and shared digital content. This modularity is a key feature that can scale through loose coupling to work across many telecommunications networks, mobile devices, and compatible operating system platforms. This is at the heart of digital business in being able to scale in an incremental and often rapid way to reach distributed customers and businesses.

Secondly, the idea of digital platforms such as public clouds, telecommunications network services, mobile app marketplaces, and enterprise application productivity tools enable collaboration and market-making around platform-supported marketplaces. We see this time and again, from the "poster children" of the internet, Google, Amazon, Facebook, Twitter, to the myriad of others that have mastered the art of platforming digital content and services to a community.

The effect of *modularity* and *platforming* potentially develops four major digital workplace strategies in the case studies we have explored. These represent alternative trajectories for digital roadmaps (see Figure 3.13).

- Encapsulated services that develop specific digital services in a workspace. Several case studies involve the development of mobile apps, data sensors that capture and provide services.
- Loose-coupled services in the workspace expand to include more digital services. Several of the case studies involving digitization of rooms, buildings, and cities included multiple digital facilities that provided a range of services for different communities and individuals.
- Expanding set of services platforms involving scaling the digital services by hosting and managing them as a digital platform. Several of the connected car, health, retail, and hospitality cases involved establishing digital platforms to collaborate customer and partner experience across the supply chain.

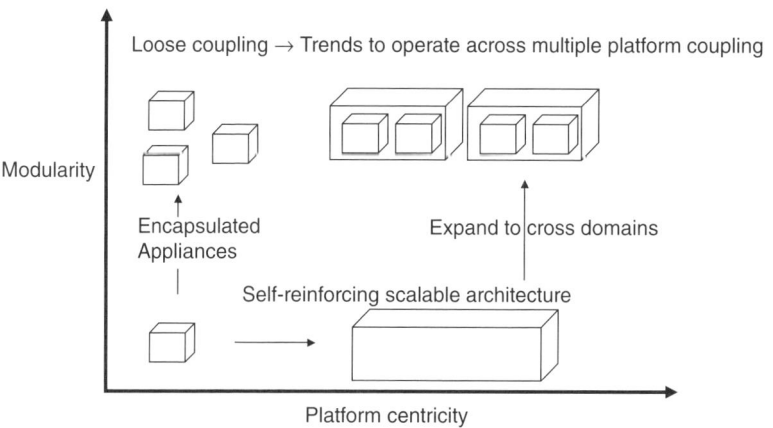

FIGURE 3.13 Modularity and platform as a core practice for digital enterprise architecture

- Operating services across multiple operating systems and platforms was seen in several connected mobile apps in government, retail, and logistics that supported a range of commercial mobile devices able to run on different operating systems.

For a practitioner, modularity and platforming are two key common practices that enable the digital workspaces and the digital enterprise to connect and build capabilities.

They also enable another key feature of multiple digital services and devices in that they can work on different levels of a digital workspace, from small physical objects to rooms, buildings, and wide connected spaces. The fact that many sensors and much software code can also be portable and embedded means that digital technologies and digital services are "clusters" that can form nested systems.[12]

Competition Moving to Ecosystem Level

You have to think of digital technologies as nested systems of systems. The resulting digital activity is many connected devices, data, and social network events that occur inside and outside the enterprise. Competition for digital connectivity and influence over the digital enterprise "has moved to the ecosystem level" (see Figure 3.14).[13]

This means that along with modularity and platforming, the extent of the digital enterprise has to consider how its own value network of digital content, connections, and services works with other physical and digital enterprises. We have previously described this as the value network ecosystem (VNE) and it is more than a digital operating model (DOM), which does not have the scope of the wider digital ecosystem we speak of here. The "ecosystem domains of concern" need to consider how the digital business model works in the wider span of digital workspaces that perhaps cross-cut many digital enterprises. This may at first sight appear complex, but in fact it is already well established in and around enterprises today. The case studies are practical proof that there are already

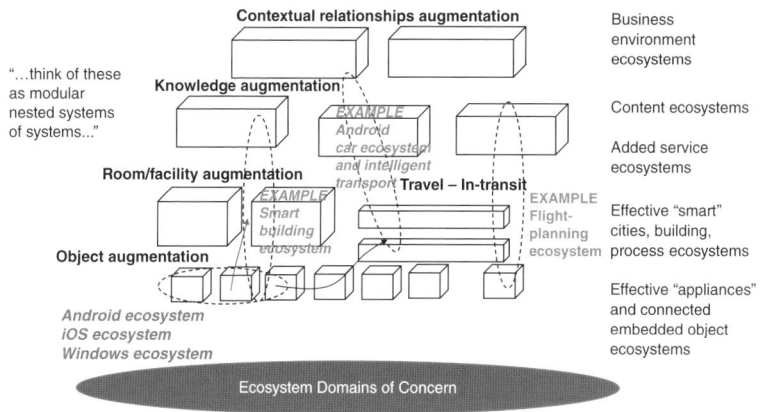

FIGURE 3.14 Competition has moved to the ecosystem level

marketplace platforms, mobile device sensors, and apps that are driving everyone from start-ups to multinational companies. Digital barriers to entry are falling as the "power of digital" is often in the hand of the consumer and the buyer, as commodification and subscriber models push technology into new on-demand services.

The Rise of Ecosystem Architecture

In defining these digital ecosystems we see many clusters of digital technologies that themselves represent systems of systems. We introduced this concept early on in the book as a key idea that has been seen in the wide variety of digital workspaces and case studies. Building a digital enterprise involves understanding the concept of clusters, or the grouping of digital technologies and the services and processes that they create:

- **Social clusters** – the groups of individuals and communities inside and outside the enterprise
- **Process clusters** – how specific tasks and work get done through a combination of human and technology or pure machine-driven automation
- **Technology clusters** – the manifold digital technologies, content, and application services

Architecting the digital enterprise becomes an awareness of how these clusters, or ecosystems, will work with the digital enterprise. This introduces the idea of a super set of architecture that we term "ecosystem architecture," which is perhaps a broader vision of systems of system engineering beyond the classic view of enterprise architecture (see Figure 3.15). This represents a set of nested architectures that together define the digital enterprise and the digital ecosystems, the digital economy, and the wider world in which we live.

Ecosystem architecture considers the continuum of architectures that might be thought of as spheres or domains of physical and virtual workspace activities.

Figure 3.16 seeks to illustrate this architectural continuum. In the enterprise technology stack, the PEC model may show specific technologies and their arrangement for component architectures and enterprise architecture.

When we introduce the notion of ecosystem architecture, this is more concerned with the clusters of digital services that represent the digital ecosystem perspective. This considers STC model issues of spatial and

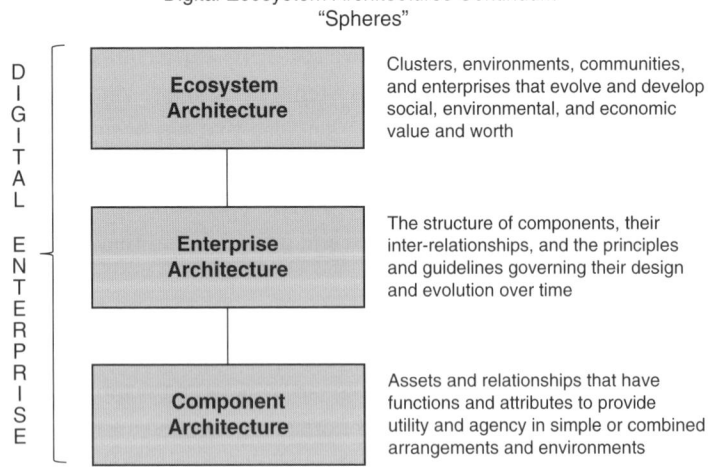

FIGURE 3.15   Ecosystem architecture continuum

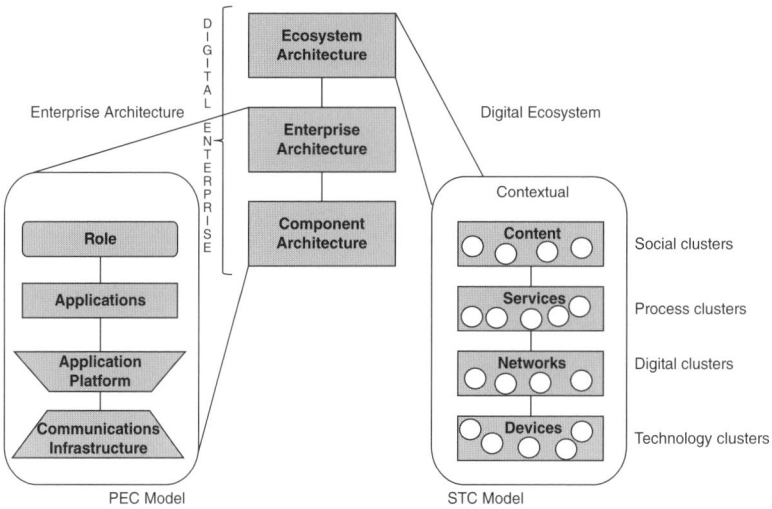

FIGURE 3.16   The role of clusters and the emergence of ecosystem architecture

temporal design of physical and virtual workspaces, and how digital content, digital services, networks, and devices work together to enable these workspaces.

The Future of Intelligent Workspaces

We have seen many examples of constructed digital workspaces and used an enterprise architecture modeling notation to define these spaces. The digital workspaces can span a number of different areas inside and outside the enterprise. The digital enterprise by definition includes its business environment, as the mobile and social networks, the cloud, data analytics, sensors, and telecommunications networks reach out beyond the four walls of the organization.

The next phase will see many digital workspaces become augmented services for "intelligence" that is applied to the workspace. As customers, employees, and enterprises increasingly use digital enterprise, they will seek further ways in which to increase automated system responses to exploit this digitization phenomenon. The line between human and machine interaction will become more blurred as information becomes aware of its context, regarding place, time, and personalization.

Digital Workspaces Pattern Catalog Example

Building the future for the digital enterprise will involve the creation and use of digital workspaces that meet the needs of participants in the enterprise and the wider ecosystem.

In the case studies and digital business models, we saw many digital workplace pattern examples. These can form the basis of a kind of digital pattern catalog showing what is possible in an enterprise.

Table 3.2 provides examples of digital services and digital workspaces that can be considered as design patterns.

The notation we have used for the pattern catalog includes:

- **Industry market** – this typically references the type of industry data identity and metadata that describe data services and objects found in that industry.
- **Class** – the term "class" refers to the type of digital platform. While there are no formal standard schema, terms such as ERP and other de facto standard naming systems can be used. In this example we use IoT to denote an Internet of Things.
- **Standards** – the architecture standards used for designing the digital workspace and impacting the interoperability and portability of the services and platforms involved. This may typically range from proprietary standards for a single operating system to open standards for shared and open source design. In our example, we have used OP3 to denote Open Standard, Open Platform 3.0 as the architecture design developed by The Open Group Standards forum. The idea is that systems and digital workspaces conforming to these standards can interoperate and support portability options.

Digital Workspaces Pattern Catalog

Industry Market	Class	Standards	Digital Workspace Service Examples	Digital Workspaces Examples	Ecosystem Clusters Examples
FMCG	IoT	OP3	Mobile services to context	Digital shop IoT platform	Social clusters
	IoT	OP3	Mobile to platform partner services	Digital VMI platform Digital franchise services	Process clusters Knowledge clusters
Hospitality	IoT	OP3	"Meeting" hospitality services	Digital "front desk" services platform	Social clusters Process clusters
	IoT	OP3	Partner "onward journey" services	Digital guest services platform	Process clusters Knowledge clusters
Financial services	IoT	OP3	Identity security assurance services	Access and Authentication Standards platform	Process–knowledge clusters
	IoT	OP3	Mobile digital wallet services	Embedded mobile platform	Social clusters Process clusters
	IoT	OP3	Partner finance added value services	Finance context analytics platform	Knowledge–process clusters
City	IoT	OP3	Sensor–control services	Digital building energy management IoT platform	Process-technology cluster
	IoT	OP3	"Visitor" market services	Digital "visitor" geospatial platform	Social clusters Knowledge clusters
ALM–PLM	IoT	OP3	Sensor – process optimization	Vehicle management platform	Social–process cluster
	IoT	OP3	Semantic product match automation	Product management platform	Knowledge Cluster Process cluster
	IoT	OP3	Dynamic software version update	Research translation platform	Process–tech clusters
	IoT	OP3	Dynamic partner services	Logistics management platform	Process cluster
eHealth	IoT	OP3	Patient care services	Mobile care platform	Social clusters Process clusters
	IoT	OP3	Clinician support services	Service support platform	Knowledge–social cluster
	IoT	OP3	Medical research	Research translation platform	Knowledge process cluster

- **Digital Workspace Services** – that support specific or many enterprise activities.
- **Digital Workspace** – supporting one or many enterprise activities and ecosystem clusters.
- **Ecosystem clusters** – groupings of open and/or proprietary social or business processes, knowledge, technology, and other actors, entities, and networks involved in the digital workspace.

Conclusion

We have seen several business models enabled by digital technologies in this closer examination of the digital enterprise.

The enterprise is more than specific solutions or individuals but a collection of capabilities that can evolve over time driven internally and externally by processes, competitors, products, and services as well as technological change.

Customer experience and digital workspace experience

A key aspect of change that we see in the case studies is the evolution of the customer experience journey as we travel through digitized environments. These connected spaces have the potential to create more immersive experiences that can transform how digital enterprise will work in the future.

The customer touchpoints along the supply chain or in a store both physically and online have become further connected by the digital workspaces that can join up different spatial and timeframes of experience. UX to CX has further developed into Digital Workspace Experience (DWX), and these together represent the digital enterprise journey (see Figure 3.17).

Toward building digital ecosystems

While digital workspaces are constructed environments, the net effect of objects, connections, and experiences is the evolution of digital

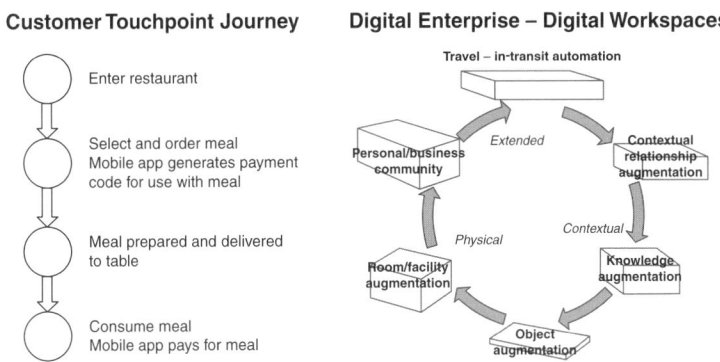

FIGURE 3.17 Transaction touchpoints to experience touchpoints

ecosystems that transcend how we might think of a modern enterprise. The earlier discussion on value chains including double- and multi-sided marketplace platforms is clearly evident in the case studies.

There is a further journey beyond the digital workspaces into the world of ecosystems, and how digital enterprises will build their digital platforms and experiences.

We have seen the early evolution of Web 2.0, with web apps and the internet now becoming more connected with mobile devices and sensors. Our case studies indicate that these digital technologies will combine into digital workspaces that form two-sided marketplaces or multi-sided marketplaces, and ultimately establish their value network ecosystems in the digital enterprise (see Figure 3.18).

Building digital enterprise design practices

How practitioners work to build digital capabilities will have an impact on the overall enterprise business model and its position and performance in its chosen marketplaces.

In the Hilton International case study we saw many examples of digital strategy and delivery that augment and enhance the guest experience and drive enterprise performance.

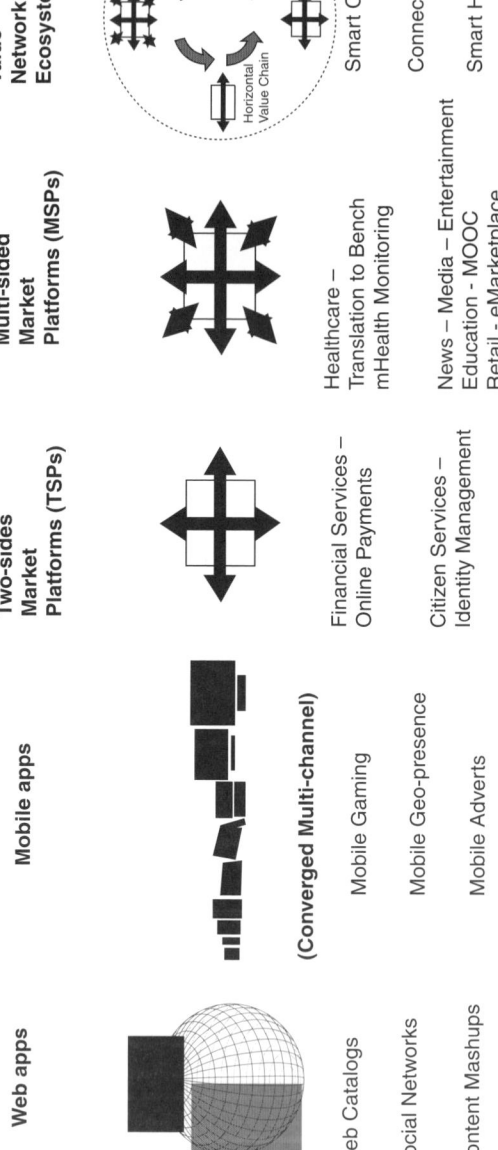

Web apps

Web Catalogs

Social Networks

Content Mashups

Mobile apps

(Converged Multi-channel)

Mobile Gaming

Mobile Geo-presence

Mobile Adverts

Two-sides Market Platforms (TSPs)

Financial Services – Online Payments

Citizen Services – Identity Management

Multi-sided Market Platforms (MSPs)

Healthcare – Translation to Bench mHealth Monitoring

News – Media – Entertainment Education - MOOC Retail - eMarketplace

Value Network Ecosystems (VNEs)

Multi-sided Platform

Vertical Value Chain

Two-sided Platform

Horizontal Value Chain

Smart City

Connected Car

Smart Hotel

FIGURE 3.18 Toward digital ecosystems

We can use this to illustrate a simple digital enterprise that brings together two major digital strategy examples: hospitality experience and hospitality delivery.

PEC model viewpoint

From the PEC model perspective of physical technology and extensions there are many opportunities for digital enhancement. Figure 3.19 provides a set of examples.

These technology solutions can be placed into the enterprise IT portfolio of the digital enterprise to create digital services, but the real power comes in understanding their alignment to the business outcomes. This is where the idea of digital workspaces considers the context of services and experience.

STC model viewpoint

The digital enterprise becomes a set of digital workspaces that can augment a physical enterprise and its relationships to the industry value chain and markets. Enterprise customer outcomes can be driven not by the technological building blocks we see in the PEC model but by how these work in the space and time locations in physical and virtual workspaces.

Both PEC and STC model perspectives are needed, but the illustration here shows that in the design of physical workplaces and digital workspaces, the consideration of user experience and customer experience is paramount.

Digital workspaces bring a experiental design approach into how the digital enterprise will operate and generate new customer experience and operational performance.

Driving outcome-based thinking with digital enterprise

In the eHotel example we saw the hospitality operational outcomes of the hotel enterprise seeking to meet guest and partner outcomes.

138

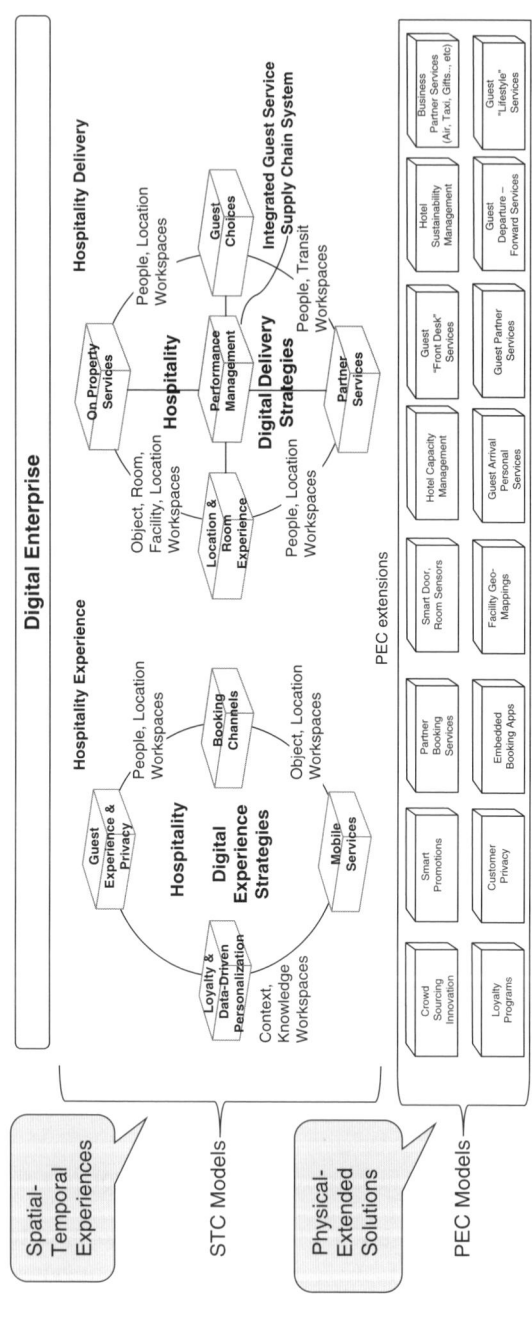

FIGURE 3.19 Digital enterprise with PEC and STC views

In the case of the digital technologies, practitioners can select and implement smart doors and room sensors, and connect these to mobile apps and front desk and onward partner services. But, as we saw in the Hilton International case study, as with others, they successfully use these in the locations and the spaces where guest and service provider come together to deliver the customer experience.

We can draw examples from the case studies showing how the outcomes of the service are driven by the design and performance of the digital enterprise. The digital workspaces can be thought of as methods that manage the contextual conditions of the enterprise and its wider ecosystems.

A useful way to consider this is by viewing the impact of contextual design on the overall performance of the enterprise (adapted from Henfridsson and Bygstad, 2013).[14]

- **Contextual conditions** – how the enterprise situation is supported by digital workspaces to enable contextual conditions. How the specific conditions enable customer, employee, and partners to be contextually relevant to the situation.
- **Mechanisms** – what specific design features do we have to drive contextual conditions and outcomes? The example in Figure 3.20 is functional design aspects.
- **Metrics** – how do we measure effective outcomes to assess the feedback and direction of the experience?
- **Outcomes** – what are the overall desired outcomes of the enterprise, the customer, and wider environment that we seek?

This experience is in the objects, rooms, facilities, employees, partners, customers, and the transport and travel that define the eHotel digital enterprise business model.

Each digital technology plays a part in the total digital workspace experience, and together they seek to increase guest satisfaction and brand loyalty, which then helps to drive value in hotel capacity and partner services.

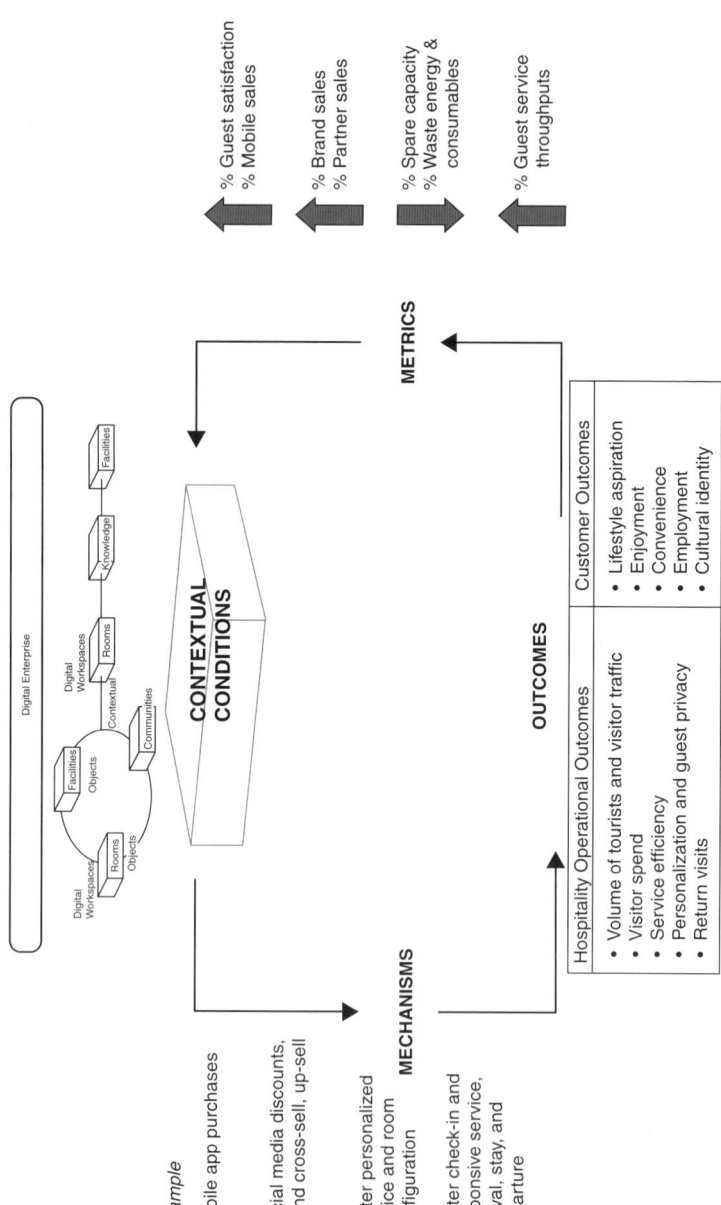

FIGURE 3.20 Designing digital workspaces that drive digital value

Measurement of economic and social value outcomes then become the key goals in measuring true digital enterprise and digital economy value (see Figure 3.20).

Chapter Summary

We have explored the concepts of digital workspaces and their position in the ideas of digital enterprise and the design of connected business.

The case studies demonstrate real examples of these practices and how they may create a new kind of reality which digital convergence is creating all around us.

The next era of technological ecosystems will need to address effective digital solutions that combine new kinds of experiential design thinking that traverse the user, customer, and living spaces.

The practitioners of today and tomorrow will be the architects of the new digital enterprise.

Notes

Introduction

1. The Open Group Definition of Terms. http://pubs.opengroup.org/architecture/togaf9-doc/arch/chap03.html.
2. Architecture has many technically focused definitions but the aim is to establish a wider description that I would describe as "ecosystem architecture." The fact is that in architecture it may not always be possible to define many systems of systems connections as some of these domains may not be under the control of the practitioner or the enterprise. The dream of "architecting the world" is only open to large companies that can have some impact and shape the market they operate in. Google, Amazon, and others are in some degree in this position, but the vast majority of enterprises are not.
3. Edwin Morris, Linda Levine, Craig Meyers, Pat Place, and Dan Plakosh, *System of Systems Interoperability (SOSI): Final Report*. April 2004. Carnegie Mellon University, https://resources .sei.cmu.edu/asset_files/TechnicalReport/2004_005_001_14375.pdf.
4. Guide to Interoperability, September 2009, *Research, Technology, and System Solutions (RTSS) Program, Software Engineering Institute*, Carnegie Mellon University.
5. J. Kallinikos, A. Aaltonen, and A. Marton, "A theory of digital objects," *First Monday*, 15 (6–7) (2010). http://firstmonday.org/ojs/index.php/fm/article/view/3033/2564.
6. L. Manovich, *The language of new media*. Cambridge, MA: MIT Press, 2001.
7. O. Henfridsson and B. Bygstad, "The generative mechanism of digital infrastructure evolution," *MIS Quarterly*, 37 (3) (2013), 907–31.
8. Y. Yoo, "Computing in everyday life: A call for research on experiential computing," *MIS Quarterly*, 34 (2) (2010), 213–31.
9. J. Kallinikos, A. Aaltonen, and A. Marton, "The ambivalent ontology of digital artifacts," *MIS Quarterly*, 37 (2) (June 2013).

10. "Measuring the information economy: The internet economy," OECD 2013. http://www.oecd.org/internet/ieconomy/measuringtheinformationeconomy.htm.
11. "OECD Internet Economy Outlook," OECD October 2012. http://www.oecd.org/sti/ieconomy/ieoutlook.htm.
12. "Global risks 2014, ninth report," Insight Report. World Economic Forum.
13. J. Kelly III and S. Hamm, *Smart machines: IBMs Watson and the era of cognitive computing*. New York: Columbia University Press, 2013.
14. Mischa Schwartz and Jeremiah Hayes, "A history of Transatlantic cables," *IEEE Communications Magazine*, 46 (9) (2008), 42–8.
15. F. A. Polkinghorn and N. F. Schlaack, "A single-sideband short-wave system for Transatlantic telephone," published in *Proc I.R.E.* (July 1935). http://alcatel-lucent.com/bstj/vol14-1935/articles/bstj14-3-489.pdf.
16. M. Newman, *Networks: An introduction*. Oxford: Oxford University Press, 2010.
17. Winston Smith, "IT spending as a percentage of revenue: Noise or real value?" March 2013, BrightHub. http://www.brighthub.com/computing/hardware/articles/123617.aspx.
18. Intel IDF14 keynote speeches, San Francisco, September 2014. http://intelstudios.edgesuite.net/idf/2014/sf/keynote/140909_bk/index.html.
19. "People are getting buzzed on these new haptic feedback devices," Co. Lab. January 10, 2014. http://www.fastcolabs.com/3024737/people-are-getting-buzzed-on-these-new-haptic-feedback-devices.
20. Vibrating timekeeper. http://www.instructables.com/id/Vibrating-Timekeeper/.
21. Apple iBeacon for Developers. https://developer.apple.com/ibeacon/.
22. Intel RealSense™. http://www.intel.com/content/www/us/en/architecture-and-technology/realsense-overview.html.
23. "Apple's secret plans for PrimeSense 3D tech hinted at by new itSeez3D iPad app," July 11, 2014. http://appleinsider.com/articles/14/07/11/apples-secret-plans-for-primesense-3d-tech-hinted-at-by-new-itseez3d-ipad-app.
24. "The phone market in 2012: A tale of two disruptions." http://www.asymco.com/2012/05/03/the-phone-market-in-2012-a-tale-of-two-disruptions/.
25. W. Visser, *The cognitive artifacts of designing*. Mahwah, NJ: Lawrence Erlbaum Associates.
26. "Design thinking – thoughts by Tim Brown." http://designthinking.ideo.com.
27. "Intel's former chief architect: Moore's law will be dead within a decade," Extreme Tech, August 2013. http://www.extremetech.com/computing/165331-intels-former-chief-architect-moores-law-will-be-dead-within-a-decade.
28. "Twitch hits one million monthly active broadcasters," Twitch the Official Blog, February 10, 2014. http://blog.twitch.tv/2014/02/twitch-hits-one-million-monthly-active-broadcasters/.
29. "A letter from the CEO," Twitch, August 25, 2014. http://blog.twitch.tv/2014/08/a-letter-from-the-ceo-august-25-2014/.

30. M. Siegel and F. Gibbons, "Amazon enters the cloud computing business," Stanford University School of Engineering, Casepublisher.com, May 20, 2008. http://web.stanford.edu/class/ee204/Publications/Amazon-EE353-2008-1.pdf.

31. R. Caldbeck, "5 marketplaces that will work in 2013," *Forbes*, January 2013. http://www.forbes.com/sites/ryancaldbeck/2013/01/10/5-marketplaces-that-work/.

32. J. Hamari, M. Sjöklint, and A. Ukkonen, "The sharing economy: Why people participate in collaborative consumption." SSRN working paper, 2013.

1 – Trends of Technological Ecosystems

1. "Digital Economy – Innovate UK," Technology Strategy Board. https://www.innovateuk.org/digital-economy.

2. "Digital Economy – Facts & Figures." Directorate General, Taxation and Customs Union. European Commission, working paper, March 2014. http://ec.europa.eu/taxation_customs/resources/documents/taxation/gen_info/good_governance_matters/digital/2014-03-13_fact_figures.pdf.

3. Internet live stats. http://www.internetlivestats.com/total-number-of-websites/.

4. Number of registered website domain names. Verisign Domain Name Industry Brief, April 2013. http://techcrunch.com/2013/04/08/internet-passes-250m-registered-top-level-domain-names/.

5. W3C Semantic Web activity, December 2013. http://www.w3.org/2001/sw/.

6. "What is Web 2.0? How Web 2.0 is defining society," about technology. http://webtrends.about.com/od/web20/a/what-is-web20.htm.

7. T. Berners-Lee, J. Hendler, and O. Lassila, "The semantic web," *Scientific American Magazine*, May 17, 2001.

8. "Web 4.0: The ultra-intelligent electronic agent is coming," *big think*, March 28, 2013. http://bigthink.com/big-think-tv/web-40-the-ultra-intelligent-electronic-agent-is-coming.

2 – Digital Workspace Concepts

1. The modern usage of the term pragmatics is attributable to the philosopher Charles Morris (1938), who was concerned to outline (after Locke and Peirce the general shape of science of signs, semiotic (or semiotic as Morris

preferred). Within semiotics, Morris distinguished three distinct branches of inquiry:

  a. Syntactics (or syntax), being the study of "the formal relation of signs to one another"
  b. Semantics, the study of "the relations of signs to the objects to which the signs are applicable" (their designate),
  c. Pragmatics, the study of "the relation of signs to interpreters" (1938:6).

2. C. W. Morris "Foundations of the Theory of Signs," *International Encyclopaedia of Unified Sciences* 1(2), Chicago: University of Chicago Press, 1938. References to W. Nöth (1990), *Handbook of Semiotics*. Bloomington, IN: Indiana University Press, 1990.
3. R. Stamper, *Information in business and administrative systems*. Cambridge: Cambridge University Press, 2001.
4. Noam Chomsky, *Syntactic structures*. Berlin: Mouton de Gruyter, 2nd edition, 2002.
5. Sematic Web, W3C. http://www.w3.org/standards/semanticweb/.
6. Tim Berners-Lee quote on Web 3.0 – Victoria Shannon, "A 'more revolutionary' Web," *International Herald Tribune*, June 26, 2006.
7. "Introducing the concepts of Web 3.0," Tweak and Trick. http://www.tweakandtrick.com/2012/05/web-30.html.
8. Chandler, D., *Semiotics: The basics*. London: Routledge, 2002.
9. Adapted from Paul Ambrose, Arkalgud Ramaprasad, and Arun Rai, "Managing thin and thinly distributed knowledge in medical genetics using the Internet," *Logistics Information Management*, 16 (3–4) (2003), 207–14.
10. The babel fish: "The Hitch-Hiker's Guide to the Galaxy," bbc.co.uk. http://www.bbc.co.uk/cult/hitchhikers/guide/babelfish.shtml.
11. J. Gaskin, N. Berente, K. Lyytinen, and Y. Yoo, "Towards generalizable sociomaterial inquiry: A computational approach for zooming in and out of sociomaterial routines," *MIS Quarterly*, 38 (3) (September 2014), 849–71.
12. Levinson, Stephen C., *Pragmatics*. Cambridge: Cambridge University Press, 1983.
13. M. H. Kennedy and S. Mahapatra, "Information analysis for effective planning and control," *Sloan Management Review*, Winter 1975, 71–83 (esp 73).
14. G. M. Marakas and J. J. Elam, "Semantic structuring in analyst acquisition and representation of facts in requirements analysis," *Information Systems Research*, 9 (1) (1998), 37–63.
15. P. Bera, A. Burton-Jones, and Y. Wand, "Research note: How semantics and pragmatics interact in understanding," *Information Systems Research*, 25 (2), 401–19.

16. "The efficient cloud: All of Salesforce runs on only 1,000 servers," Techcrunch, March 23, 2009. http://techcrunch.com/2009/03/23/the-efficient-cloud-all-of-salesforce-runs-on-only-1000-servers/.

17. Google Data Centers locations. http://www.google.co.uk/about/datacenters/inside/locations/.

18. "50 things you didn't know about Google," UK.complex.com, February 22, 2013. http://uk.complex.com/pop-culture/2013/02/50-things-you-didnt-know-about-google/20-petabytes.

19. "Google: There are 900 million Android devices activated," Business Insider, May 15, 2013. http://www.businessinsider.com/900-million-android-devices-in-2013-2013-5.

20. "Google play hits one million Android apps," readwrite, July 24, 2013. http://readwrite.com/2013/07/24/google-play-hits-one-million-android-apps.

21. M. van Rijmenam, "Walmart makes big data part of its DNA," Smart Data Collective, March 17, 2013. http://smartdatacollective.com/bigdatastartups/111681/walmart-makes-big-data-part-its-social-media.

22. R. Moss, "Walmart.com's improved search engine powered by 'Social Genome'," retailwire, September 10, 2012. http://www.retailwire.com/discussion/16260/walmart-coms-improved-search-engine-powered-by-social-genome.

23. "Walmart get on the shelf." https://getontheshelf.walmart.com/.

24. G. Kearns, "Innovative strategies to leverage big data – Drive co-brand and core business sales," MasterCard, Group Executive, Information Services, March 19, 2013. http://www.slideshare.net/morellimarc/mastercard-big-data-2013.

25. "M2M applications: Are connected cars the new smartphones?" Mformation Blog, n.d., http://www.mformation.com/mformation-news/mformation_blog/m2m-applications-connected-cars-new-smartphones/?utm_source=twitter&utm_medium=social&utm_content=4242079#.VBWob_ldV8F.

26. "Data, data everywhere," The Economist (February 25, 2010). http://www.economist.com/node/15557443.

27. P. Delort, OECD ICCP Technology Foresight Forum, 2012. http://www.oecd.org/sti/ieconomy/Session_3_Delort.pdf#page=6.

28. D. Goodman, "This week in the internet of things: Connected cars, smart home controls, gesture-based sensors and big data processing. Skyhook Wireless, March 14, 2014. http://blog.skyhookwireless.com/this-week-in-the-internet-of-things-connected-cars-smart-home-controls-gesture-based-sensors-and-big-data-processing-.

29. Fujitsu, "Solving the big dilemma of big data." http://www.fujitsu.com/downloads/TEL/fnc/whitepapers/BigDatawp.pdf.

30. David Thornburn, "Web of paradox." Cited in his introduction to the conference: Democracy and Digital Media and subsequently published in American

Prospect, September–October 1998, 78–80. http://web.mit.edu/comm-forum/papers/thorburn-web.html.

31. Live Blog: World Retail Congress, October 8, 2013, Finextra. http://www.finextra.com/news/fullstory.aspx?newsitemid=25289&topic=innovation.

32. "BPM is NOT software engineering," bpm.com, November 30, 2008. http://www.bpm.com/bpm-is-not-software-engineering.html.

33. Artificial intelligence programming language. http://www.britannica.com/EBchecked/topic/1473945/artificial-intelligence-programming-language#ref1069879.

34. Allan Gottlieb and George S. Almasi, *Highly parallel computing*. Redwood City, CA: Benjamin/Cummings, 1989.

35. D. Shiffman, "The nature of code: Simulating natural systems with processing, December 13, 2012, Amazon. http://natureofcode.com/book/chapter-10-neural-networks/.

36. J. Kelly III and S. Hamm, *Smart machines: IBM's Watson and the era of cognitive computing*. New York: Columbia University Press, 2013.

37. G. Beni and J. Wang, "Swarm intelligence in cellular robotic systems." Proceedings of the NATO Advanced Workshop on Robots and Biological Systems, Tuscany, Italy, June 26–30, 1989.

38. J. Bartlett, "No, Eugene didn't pass the Turing Test – but he will soon," *Daily Telegraph*, June 21, 2014. http://blogs.telegraph.co.uk/technology/jamiebartlett/100013858/no-eugene-didnt-pass-the-turing-test-but-he-will-soon/.

39. Hiroshi Ishiguro, "Android science," Cognitive Science Society, Osaka, 2005.

40. A. Adshead, "Big data storage: Defining big data and the type of storage it needs," *Computer Weekly* (April 2013). http://www.computerweekly.com/podcast/Big-data-storage-Defining-big-data-and-the-type-of-storage-it-needs.

41. C. Sliwa, "Understanding stripped-down hyperscale storage for big data use cases," TechTarget Search Storage (March 2013). http://searchstorage.techtarget.com/podcast/Understanding-stripped-down-hyperscale-storage-for-big-data-use-cases.

42. Chris Anderson, "The Long Tail," 2004–14. http://www.longtail.com/about.html.

3 – Design Practices in the Digital Enterprise

1. "Global travel & tourism industry defies economic uncertainty by outperforming the global economy in 2012 – and predicted to do it again in 2013." World Travel and Tourism Council. http://www.hospitalitynet.org/news/4059643.html.

2. Hilton International global website. http://www.hiltonworldwide.com/about/.
3. Second quarter business results – Hilton International, June 30, 2014. http://www.businesswire.com/news/home/20140801005062/en/Hilton-Worldwide-Reports-Strong-Quarter-2014-Results#.VDFA-_IdWSo.
4. "Hilton revolutionizes hotel experience with digital check-in, room selection and customization, and check-out across 650,000-plus rooms at more than 4,000 properties worldwide," Hilton International press release, July 28, 2014. http://news.hiltonworldwide.com/index.cfm/newsroom/detail/27192.
5. Hilton International global privacy policy – code of practice. http://hhonors3.hilton.com/en/promotions/privacy-policy/english.html.
6. Partnership development for Hilton Hotels – an open innovation solution to help Hilton Hotels develop its business. http://www.ideaconnection.com/open-innovation-success/Partnership-Development-for-Hilton-Hotels-00140.html.
7. FlyerTalk. http://www.flyertalk.com/.
8. ArchiMate®, an Open Group Standard, is an open and independent modeling language for enterprise architecture. http://www.opengroup.org/subjectareas/enterprise/archimate.
9. ArchiMate® Download Center. http://www.opengroup.org/archimate/downloads.htm.
10. Technology Reference Model TRM, Figure 43-1, TOGAF 9, The Open Group. http://pubs.opengroup.org/architecture/togaf9-doc/arch/chap43.html.
11. The Open Group Open Platform 3™ forum. http://www.opengroup.org/subjectareas/platform3.0.
12. Y. Yoo, O. Henfridsson, and K. Lyytinen, "The new organizing logic of digital innovation: An agenda for information systems research," *Journal of Information Systems Research*, 21 (4) (December 2010), 724–35. http://dl.acm.org/citation.cfm?id=1923786.
13. Youngjin Yoo, "Digitization and unbounded innovation," Slideshare http://www.slideshare.net/yxy23yoo.
14. O. Henfridsson and B. Bygstad, "The generative mechanisms of digital infrastructure evolution," *MIS Quarterly*, 37 (3) (2013), 907–31. http://misq.org/the-generative-mechanisms-of-digital-infrastructure-evolution.html?SID=7ntdq5gqhaegskupgqomh3l9j4.

International Technical and Business Standards Bodies and Suggested Further Reading

A selection of active standards bodies exist in the field of digital enterprise and digital ecosystems development. There are many active initiatives; the aim here is to provide an illustration of some of the key themes.

You can find details of these at http://building-the-digital-enterprise.com/international-technical-and-business-standards-bodies-and-suggested-futher-reading.

Index

Printed and bound by CPI Group (UK) Ltd, Croydon, CR0 4YY